'*The Holy Spirit Handboc*
road

'Bill writes with insight
Spirit. Read on and discover how the Holy Spirit can
transform your life'
Andrew McNeil, Senior Pastor
Birmingham Vineyard

'Bill is full of the Holy Spirit and overflowing with
great joy. By tapping into his wisdom and insights in
this book you are sure to encounter God in a special
way. May you receive a fresh baptism of the Holy
Spirit as you read this powerful book'
Jennifer A. Miskov, Ph.D
Author and Founding Director, Destiny House
Redding, California

'Beautifully authentic because it is the journey the
author has walked through and experienced for himself
over many years'
Andrew Leakey, Team Leader, in:courage

'We testify to the value and effectiveness of this book'
Tom and Alison Husbands
Founding Directors, Dalitso Trust, Malawi

'This book is born out of Bill's many years of
experience training church leaders in Africa and
around the world. I commend it to those who want an
informative, practical and easy-to-use reference book
on what the Bible teaches about the Holy Spirit'
Professor Allan Heaton Anderson
University of Birmingham

Bill Dixon grew up in the rural Cotswolds, when the sight of a car was a rare thing. He prepared for the Baptist Ministry at Bristol Baptist College and studied theology at Bristol University. He led churches in Bristol and inner city Birmingham for forty years, also serving on the Prison Parole Board and as Chairman of Mercian Housing Association. After getting Prime Minister Harold Wilson involved with a community regeneration initiative in Birmingham, Bill turned his attention to the growth of the local church. He was instrumental, with others, in introducing the Vineyard Church to Birmingham. This led to a sabbatical at Newport Beach, California, followed by extensive travel in South Africa, Malawi, Mozambique, Siberia, Iraq, Albania, and Lebanon, to deliver mentoring projects. Bill remains a trustee of Birmingham Vineyard Church. He is married to Jennifer and they have one remaining son, Peter.

The Holy Spirit

Handbook

Bill Dixon

TRANSFORMING CITIES

First published in Great Britain by Transforming Cities in 2015

www.transformingcities.co.uk

The Holy Spirit Handbook is the result of work undertaken by Bill Dixon
for the Dalitso Trust operating in Malawi. It is part of a series of
Handbooks under the programme 'Follow Me', helping to equip and
empower local Christian leadership. It is available for translation into
other languages. **www.dalitsotrust.org**

Other Handbooks in the series include:

Basic Christian Leadership
Chosen of God: The Chichewa Speaking People
The Leader's Handbook
Basic Christian Theology
Occasional Papers

To the Malingunde team in Malawi:
Chippo, Cecil, Patterson, Janet, Rhodess, Japhael,
Jameson, Bisfat, Bazilio, Lonely, Fanny,
and those yet to come

Contents

Introduction

The key to understanding the Holy Spirit is to grasp the fact that He is everything to the believer now that Jesus was to the disciples then.

In the beginning there was God; Father, Son and Holy Spirit. This awesome triumvirate spoke into being the created order that we know as our universe (and maybe many more). On planet earth He set the crown of his creation, mankind, who had the freedom to reciprocate the love that motivated His creation. However it was not long before mankind chose the centre stage for his own self and put all life's future days and generations in jeopardy. To redeem, recreate and re-establish this Eden, God set in place through law, covenant and prophet, ways and means to woo His first love, seeking to restore man's original status. Alas nothing was ever effectively accomplished.

It was the intervention of God in the nature of His Son, known to us as Jesus Christ, that achieved what law, covenant and prophet could not. Salvation through His death upon the cross accomplished the reconciliation of all things in and through Him. The kingdom of God broke in again through His resurrection but not in all its completeness, for kingdom consummation is yet to come.

The arrival of the Holy Spirit, whilst the Jewish nation busily celebrated the feast of Pentecost, was the culmination of Christ's ministry. Returning to the Father He asked for the fulfillment of the promise that another, like Him, would be sent to be with us forever.

In these days of tumultuous disorder with chaos of gargantuan proportions abounding, there live and thrive communities of the followers of Jesus, bearing a multiplicity of names and none, who, through the presence and the power of the Holy Spirit, seek to participate in the kingdom's coming, remaining faithful to the end.

In these pages an attempt is made to answer from the scriptures the question of who the Holy Spirit is and what His ministry is. My understanding is that He has been sent so that we, in company with all other followers, will join the celebration when, 'The kingdom of the world has become the kingdom of our Lord and of His Christ, and He will reign for ever and ever.' (Revelation 11:15).

Part 1
The Scripture's unfolding revelation of the Holy Spirit and His ministry

1: Holy Spirit activity in the Old Testament

From beginning to end, the pages of the Bible are infused with the presence of the Holy Spirit. From the human perspective He has an escalating role in the unfolding drama of mankind's redemption.

Genesis 1:2. The Spirit BROODED on the waters.
'Now the earth was formless and empty, darkness was over the surface of the deep, and the Spirit of God was hovering over the waters.'
Here the Holy Spirit is seen as the initiator and the inaugurator in the activity of creation.

Judges 13:24-25, 16:28-30. The Spirit was the POWER of Samson.
'The woman gave birth to a boy and named him Samson. He grew and the Lord blessed him, and the Spirit of the Lord began to stir him while he was in Mahaneh Dan, between Zorah and Eshtaol.'
'Then Samson prayed to the Lord, "O Sovereign Lord, remember me. O God, please strengthen me just once more, and let me with one blow get revenge on the Philistines for my two eyes." Then Samson reached toward the two central pillars on which the

temple stood. Bracing himself against them, his right hand on the one and his left hand on the other, Samson said, "Let me die with the Philistines!" Then he pushed with all his might, and down came the temple on the rulers and all the people in it. Thus he killed many more when he died than while he lived.'

The Holy Spirit here is focused down on a single human frame which then bears all the extraordinary power and ability of Almighty God.

1 Samuel 16:13. The Spirit, was the POWER and ANOINTING of David.

'So Samuel took the horn of oil and anointed him in the presence of his brothers, and from that day on the Spirit of the LORD came upon David in power. Samuel then went to Ramah.'

The result of the Lord's directive is that David is selected to be the recipient of the Spirit of the Lord to enable him both to be the extraordinary person he was and to accomplish the outstanding deeds ordained for him by God.

1 Kings 3:5, 9-14. The Spirit, the WISDOM of Solomon.

'At Gibeon the LORD appeared to Solomon during the night in a dream, and God said, "Ask for whatever you want me to give you."

"So give your servant a discerning heart to govern your people and to distinguish between right and wrong. For who is able to govern this great people of yours?"

The Lord was pleased that Solomon had asked for this. So God said to him, "Since you have asked for this and not for long life or wealth for yourself, nor have asked for the death of your enemies but for discernment in administering justice, I will do what you have asked. I will give you a wise and discerning heart, so that there will never have been anyone like you, nor will there ever be. Moreover, I will give you what you have not asked for - both riches and honour - so that in your lifetime you will have no equal among kings. And if you walk in my ways and obey my statutes and commands as David your father did, I will give you a long life.'"

Divine wisdom is manifest through a human mind as Solomon is the recipient of the Holy Spirit.

Conclusion

These examples clearly indicate that the activity of the Holy Spirit as indwelling all God's children individually had not yet arrived. The Holy Spirit came mightily upon individuals but for a limited task or season. We shall see a new dimension of His presence as promise is fulfilled in new and dramatic ways as our story continues. The progenitor of creation, The Holy Spirit, is successively revealed as indweller, empowerer and accomplisher of divine activity in human frailty.

2: Holy Spirit activity in the life of Jesus

Matthew 1:18. Jesus CONCEIVED by the Holy Spirit.
'This is how the birth of Jesus Christ came about: His mother Mary was pledged to be married to Joseph, but before they came together, she was found to be with child through the Holy Spirit.'

The Spirit, is the EQUIPPER of Jesus:

Matthew 3:13-17. 'Then Jesus came from Galilee to the Jordan to be baptised by John. But John tried to deter him, saying, "I need to be baptised by you, and do you come to me?"

Jesus replied, "Let it be so now; it is proper for us to do this to fulfill all righteousness." Then John consented.

As soon as Jesus was baptised, he went up out of the water. At that moment heaven was opened, and he saw the Spirit of God descending like a dove and lighting on him. And a voice from heaven said, "This is my Son, whom I love; with him I am well pleased."'

Mark 1:9-11. 'At that time Jesus came from Nazareth in Galilee and was baptised by John in the Jordan. As Jesus was coming up out of the water, he saw heaven being torn open and the Spirit descending on him like a dove. And a voice came from heaven: "You are my Son, whom I love; with you I am well pleased."'

Luke 3:21-22. 'When all the people were being baptised, Jesus was baptised too. And as he was praying, heaven was opened and the Holy Spirit descended on him in bodily form like a dove. And a voice came from heaven: "You are my Son, whom I love; with you I am well pleased."'

John 1:32-34. 'Then John gave this testimony: "I saw the Spirit come down from heaven as a dove and remain on him. I would not have known him, except that the one who sent me to baptise with water told me, "The man on whom you see the Spirit come down and remain is he who will baptise with the Holy Spirit." I have seen and I testify that this is the Son of God."'

Luke 4:1. 'Jesus, full of the Holy Spirit, returned from the Jordan and was led by the Spirit in the desert.'

Luke 4:14. 'Jesus returned to Galilee in the power of the Spirit, and news about him spread through the whole countryside.'

Luke 4:18-19. Sees Jesus declare that he is the inheritor of the prophecy of Isaiah 61:1-2.

"The Spirit of the Lord is on me,
because he has anointed me
to preach good news to the poor.
He has sent me to proclaim freedom for the prisoners
and recovery of sight for the blind,
to release the oppressed,

to proclaim the year of the Lord's favour."

Conclusion

In these scriptures we are seeing the emergence of the prototype of the NEW ADAM. The OLD ADAM conceded and continues to concede all the inadequacies of 'fallen' creation. The redemptive activity of God emerges as the Son, the New Adam, and the Holy Spirit begin the process of the reclamation of all that was lost in the Fall. All the disasters initiated through Adam, which are still today being played out in the everyday life of the world, are being reversed and restored.

3: John's water baptism and Jesus' Holy Spirit baptism

The Biblical evidence is that JOHN THE BAPTIST baptises with/in WATER and his testimony is that JESUS baptises with/in the HOLY SPIRIT.

John's testimony

Matthew 3:11. "I baptise you with water for repentance. But after me will come one who is more powerful than I, whose sandals I am not fit to carry. He will baptise you with the Holy Spirit and with fire."

Mark 1:8. "I baptise you with water, but he will baptise you with the Holy Spirit."

Luke 3:16. 'John answered them all, "I baptise you with water. But one more powerful than I will come, the thongs of whose sandals I am not worthy to untie. He will baptise you with the Holy Spirit and with fire."'

John 1:31, 33. "I myself did not know him, but the reason I came baptising with water was that he might be revealed to Israel."

"I would not have known him, except that the one who sent me to baptise with water told me, 'The man on whom you see the Spirit come down and remain is he who will baptise with the Holy Spirit.""

Jesus' testimony

Acts 1:5
Acts 1:5 "For John baptised with water, but in a few days you will be baptised with the Holy Spirit."

The real meaning of both these events would come to light as the days and years played out just as the scriptures testify.

Matthew 21:25
"John's baptism - where did it come from? Was it from heaven, or from men?"

Mark 11:30
"John's baptism - was it from heaven, or from men? Tell me!"

Luke 20:4
"John's baptism - was it from heaven, or from men?"

Act's 19:3
So Paul asked, "Then what baptism did you receive?"

"John's baptism," they replied.

Acts 19:4
Paul said, "John's baptism was a baptism of repentance. He told the people to believe in the one coming after him, that is, in Jesus."

All was soon to be revealed and we owe it to Luke,

who having written his gospel continued the story in the Acts of the Apostles.

Acts 1:1-5.

'In my former book, Theophilus, I wrote about all that Jesus began to do and to teach until the day he was taken up to heaven, after giving instructions through the Holy Spirit to the apostles he had chosen. After his suffering, he showed himself to these men and gave many convincing proofs that he was alive. He appeared to them over a period of forty days and spoke about the kingdom of God. On one occasion, while he was eating with them, he gave them this command: "Do not leave Jerusalem, but wait for the gift my Father promised, which you have heard me speak about. For John baptised with water, but in a few days you will be baptised with the Holy Spirit."'

Conclusion

Here the unequivocal evidence of scripture regarding the testimony of both John the Baptist and Jesus concerning Holy Spirit baptism is set out. This has not always been either taught or understood among the differing communities of believers. It is essential if we are to grow in our understanding, both of the person and the work of the Holy Spirit, that we understand these scriptural foundations.

4: The first recorded mass baptism in the Holy Spirit

The inauguration of the Jewish Feast of Weeks is described in **Exodus 34:22**:

'Celebrate the Feast of Weeks with the first fruits of the wheat harvest, and the Feast of Ingathering at the turn of the year.'

Deuteronomy 16:9-10 is a further reminder.

'Count off seven weeks from the time you begin to put the sickle to the standing grain. Then celebrate the Feast of Weeks to the LORD your God by giving a freewill offering in proportion to the blessings the LORD your God has given you.'

This celebration became known as the Festival of Pentecost, still marked by the Jews to this day. It was whilst the Jews were celebrating this that the following happened:

Acts 2:1-4. 'When the day of Pentecost came, they were all together in one place. Suddenly a sound like the blowing of a violent wind came from heaven and filled the whole house where they were sitting. They saw what seemed to be tongues of fire that separated and came to rest on each of them. All of them were filled with the Holy Spirit and began to speak in other tongues as the Spirit enabled them.'

Clearly Jesus had kept his word recorded in John

14:15-21. "If you love me, you will obey what I command. And I will ask the Father, and he will give you another Counsellor to be with you forever - the Spirit of truth. The world cannot accept him, because it neither sees him nor knows him. But you know him, for he lives with you and will be in you. I will not leave you as orphans; I will come to you. Before long, the world will not see me anymore, but you will see me. Because I live, you also will live. On that day you will realize that I am in my Father, and you are in me, and I am in you. Whoever has my commands and obeys them, he is the one who loves me. He who loves me will be loved by my Father, and I too will love him and show myself to him."

The Holy Spirit had arrived in a way no one was expecting. However, it was revealed to Peter by the Holy Spirit that this was the fulfillment of Joel 2:28-29:

'This is what was spoken by the prophet Joel:
"And afterward,
I will pour out my Spirit on all people.
Your sons and daughters will prophesy,
your old men will dream dreams,
your young men will see visions.
Even on my servants, both men and women,
I will pour out my Spirit in those days."'

The inquiring multitude, listening to Peter's explanation, asked a dangerous question, dangerous in the sense of the consequences that could follow if they responded!

Acts 2:36-37. "Therefore let all Israel be assured of

this: God has made this Jesus, whom you crucified, both Lord and Christ."

When the people heard this, they were cut to the heart and said to Peter and the other apostles, "Brothers, what shall we do?"

Acts 2:38-41. 'Peter replied, "Repent and be baptised, every one of you, in the name of Jesus Christ for the forgiveness of your sins. And you will receive the gift of the Holy Spirit. The promise is for you and your children and for all who are far off - for all whom the Lord our God will call."

With many other words he warned them; and he pleaded with them, "Save yourselves from this corrupt generation." Those who accepted his message were baptised, and about three thousand were added to their number that day.'

How long it might have taken the apostles to baptise 3000 in water is one thing but it only took Jesus a second to baptise them in the Holy Spirit!

Remember, the reason God chose the occasion of this festival was not accidental it was intentional. Jews had gathered from all over the known world. They had come together, and so they had to go home! Thousands went home as totally changed people, for they were now Jews who had been baptised in water and the Holy Spirit. They spread out over the nations and later, wherever the apostles would go to the nations they would find groups of God fearing people, some baptised in water, some in the Spirit, but all ready to begin to be the Church, the new congregation of the King.

5: Subsequent mass baptisms in the New Testament

Acts 4:31. 'After they prayed, the place where they were meeting was shaken. And they were all filled with the Holy Spirit and spoke the word of God boldly.'

Acts 8:14-17. 'When the apostles in Jerusalem heard that Samaria had accepted the word of God, they sent Peter and John to them. When they arrived, they prayed for them that they might receive the Holy Spirit, because the Holy Spirit had not yet come upon any of them; they had simply been baptised into the name of the Lord Jesus. Then Peter and John placed their hands on them, and they received the Holy Spirit.'

Acts 10:44-48. 'While Peter was still speaking these words, the Holy Spirit came on all who heard the message. The circumcised believers who had come with Peter were astonished that the gift of the Holy Spirit had been poured out even on the Gentiles. For they heard them speaking in tongues and praising God.
Then Peter said, "Can anyone keep these people from being baptised with water? They have received the Holy Spirit just as we have." So he ordered that they be baptised in the name of Jesus Christ. Then they asked Peter to stay with them for a few days.'

Confusing? Yes, some were baptised with water first and some were baptised by the Holy Spirit first! It doesn't seem to matter to God which order is followed as long as the baptisms take place.

Acts 11:26. 'So for a whole year Barnabas and Saul met with the church and taught great numbers of people. The disciples were called Christians first at Antioch.'

It looks as though Christians are those who are born of water and the Spirit!

Personally when I was baptised in the Holy Spirit I was alone but I have been present when hundreds have been baptised in a moment.

Now we are dramatically made aware that the will of God, manifest in the incarnation of his Son, Jesus, through his crucifixion and resurrection and ascension, climaxes in the pouring out of the Holy Spirit on all believers. A reading of the remainder of the New Testament confirms the work of the Holy Spirit to create, build and bring the Church restored in perfection, back to the Father as the gift (bride) of his dear Son.

Jude 1:24. 'To him who is able to keep you from falling and to present you before his glorious presence without fault and with great joy - to the only God our saviour be glory, majesty, power and authority, through Jesus Christ our Lord, before all ages, now and forevermore! Amen.'

There is a hymn we sing from time to time, written

by Keith Green, which expresses the truth we have been exploring in a helpful and concise way:

There is a redeemer,
Jesus, God's own Son,
Precious Lamb of God, Messiah,
Holy One,

Jesus my redeemer,
Name above all names,
Precious Lamb of God, Messiah,
Oh, for sinners slain.

Thank you oh my Father,
For giving us Your Son,
And leaving Your Spirit,
'Til the work on Earth is done.

When I stand in Glory,
I will see His face,
And there I'll serve my King forever,
In that Holy Place.

Thank you oh my Father,
For giving us Your Son,
And leaving Your Spirit,
'Til the work on Earth is done.

There is a redeemer,
Jesus, God's own Son,
Precious Lamb of God, Messiah,
Holy One,

Thank you oh my Father,

For giving us Your Son,
And leaving Your Spirit,
'Til the work on Earth is done.

6: Understanding the Holy Spirit and His work in a new way

Yes, He is the third person of the Trinity. Father, Son, and Holy Spirit. One God.

No, He is not a feeling, not an influence, not a bit of God in me.

Yes, the Holy Spirit is 'he', a person, not an 'it'.

The significance of this is that we can have a living, vibrant, relationship with a person.

John 14:16–17. 'I will ask the Father, and he will give you another Counsellor to be with you forever - the Spirit of truth. The world cannot accept him, because it neither sees him nor knows him. But you know him, for he lives with you and will be in you.'

Jesus says, 'I will ask the Father, and He will give you another Counsellor to be with you forever, the spirit of truth. The word 'another' in the Greek language has the weight of 'another like me.'
If you want to know who the Holy Spirit is like, you look at Jesus.

It is now possible to describe a relationship with God as, Father, Son, and Holy Spirit.

What are the characteristics of such a relationship? What does it look like?

John 16:14-15. 'He will bring glory to me by taking from what is mine and making it known to you. All that belongs to the Father is mine. That is why I said the Spirit will take from what is mine and make it known to you.'

His job is to keep us on track with Jesus by constantly reminding us of everything Jesus said and did. To constantly reveal the truth of all Jesus said and did.

His ministry is to point us to Jesus (away from himself), and the Ministry of Jesus is to show us the Father.

Remember: Everything that Jesus was to the disciples then, the Holy Spirit is to us now.

7: The Holy Spirit as teacher, counsellor, instructor, helper, and advocate

These are the characteristics that we experience as the Holy Spirit lives in and through us.

Teacher

Acts 1:1-2. "In my former book, Theophilus, I wrote about all that Jesus began to do and to teach until the day he was taken up to heaven, after giving instructions through the Holy Spirit to the apostles he had chosen."

These are an easily overlooked couple of verses in Luke's introduction to Part 2 of his story of the birth and growth of the church. In an almost off handed way we get an insight into what Jesus and the disciples were up to in the 40 days between the time of Jesus' resurrection and his ascension. It was an intense time of teaching by Jesus, about the Holy Spirit and the kingdom. It would not make too much sense to the disciples until after the coming of the Holy Spirit at Pentecost. It certainly makes clear what Jesus was talking about in this verse John records for us. John 14:26. "But the Counsellor, the Holy Spirit, whom the Father will send in my name, will teach you all things and will remind you of everything I have said to you."

Whenever we engage with the Bible we should

always invite the Holy Spirit to be our teacher, highlighting for us the things the Spirit wants us to comprehend in any given situation. The Holy Spirit takes the things of Jesus and makes them real to us. The finest example of this for me is when Peter combats the idea that the disciples were drunk by drawing attention to the prophet Joel who foretold these very things happening!

I love it when the Holy Spirit does that sort of thing when I am teaching or preaching. He highlights a scripture that is deep in the recesses of my mind, brings it to the fore and it is God's word for the moment. I recall having a strong conviction that I should preach on the theme, 'The Emerging Prophetic Church'. I also felt as if I was given the book of Zechariah as the scripture to use. Not being too familiar with that book I began to study it more carefully. The first Sunday came and I wondered where the message had come from; it was hard to stop. For the next five Sundays the Holy Spirit kept giving me the truths to teach and I knew it was all in a league beyond me! There were those who said that it was the finest set of sermons they had ever heard me preach. It had little to do with me. I was left indebted to the Holy Spirit as I had never been before. Oh that this happened on a regular basis! What I had discovered was what it meant to be a channel of the Holy Spirit. He taught me as I preached.

Counsellor

The Holy Spirit is the one who is best placed to give guidance on any level of our personal life. The fact is, of course, there is no one who knows us so intimately, cares for us more profoundly, and loves us more comprehensively.

To turn to the Holy Spirit is to access the one who is able to dispense the wisdom and knowledge of God as it applies to us and through us to others.

Instructor

When I began my Trade Training in The Royal Air Force I had an Instructor who taught me how to care for three types of aircraft engines: air cooled, liquid cooled, and pure jet. It was his responsibility to pass on to me, not only all the knowledge he possessed but also all the experience he had accrued over his lifetime. He did a good job because I passed out with honours.

When I apply this to my relationship with the Holy Spirit I see the same thing taking place. The Holy Spirit seeks to impart to me all His knowledge about Jesus, but more than that, His desire is to share with me all His experience. How good a job He does is not dependent solely on Him but it also depends on my willingness to allow Him to have control in and over my life.

Helper

As helper, the Holy Spirit is the one who comes alongside us to make things easier for us, to benefit us in some way, to serve us and to ensure that we are never left to our own devices. He is an inner and outer resource who makes us, who are incomplete, complete in him.

I have lost count of the times that our vehicles have

broken down on the roads in Malawi and Mozambique. However, there has never been one occasion when someone has not come along to help us and set us on our way again. A great example of how the Holy Spirit relates to us is as He comes along side us, except that He is there when we have not broken down as well!

Advocate

To have one who stands along side and publicly supports us, is to experience the Holy Spirit. He is the one who pleads our cause. When sin has had its devastating effect upon us the Holy Spirit pleads our cause, not making excuses, but pointing, as always to Jesus and reminding Him that it is His prerogative to forgive when we ask. When looking for someone to stand up for him the believer turns to the Holy Spirit, whose ministry is to do just that!

God exists and lives in relationship as Father, Son and Holy Spirit. As His creation, part of being made in His image is that we too exist to live in relationship with Him. What a glorious truth that ours is the privilege of being wooed by the Spirit, to fall in love with Jesus and find our inheritance in the Father. What more could we want, what more do we need?

Part 2
The activity of the Holy Spirit in the life of the believer

1: Baptism in the Holy Spirit

Baptism in the Holy Spirit is God's ambition for every believer so that together believers can enjoy the privilege of participating in His work of creating, building and perfecting the Church and participating in the inauguration of the kingdom.

We are now ready to explore the following: how to be baptised in the Holy Spirit; what the gifts are He gives us to do His work; what fruit the Spirit produces in us; and the destiny prepared for us with Him.

It is good to be reminded that the first step of obedience in following Jesus is to be baptised by immersion in water. That is a once in a lifetime experience. The next step is to seek baptism in the Holy Spirit by Jesus Himself and to realise that this is a continuous experience and not once in a lifetime.

2: How Jesus baptises in the Holy Spirit

John 14:16-21 reads as follows; "And I will ask the Father, and he will give you another Counsellor to be with you forever - the Spirit of truth. The world cannot accept him, because it neither sees him nor knows him. But you know him, for he lives with you and will be in you. I will not leave you as orphans; I will come to you. Before long, the world will not see me anymore, but you will see me. Because I live, you also will live. On that day you will realise that I am in my Father, and you are in me, and I am in you. Whoever has my commands and obeys them, he is the one who loves me. He who loves me will be loved by my Father, and I too will love him and show myself to him."

The first thing to realise is that this is a biblical promise and biblical promises are not broken. As Peter said in his first sermon, "This is that," - as the late John Wimber was so fond of quoting; this is that of which Joel prophesied, 2:28-32:

'And afterward,
I will pour out my Spirit on all people.
Your sons and daughters will prophesy,
your old men will dream dreams,
your young men will see visions.
Even on my servants, both men and women,
I will pour out my Spirit in those days.
I will show wonders in the heavens
and on the earth,
blood and fire and billows of smoke.
The sun will be turned to darkness

and the moon to blood
before the coming of the great and dreadful day of
the LORD.
And everyone who calls
on the name of the LORD will be saved;
for on Mount Zion and in Jerusalem
there will be deliverance,
as the LORD has said,
among the survivors
whom the LORD calls.'

John 7:37. 'On the last and greatest day of the
Feast, Jesus stood and said in a loud voice, "If anyone
is thirsty, let him come to me and drink. Whoever
believes in me, as the Scripture has said, streams of
living water will flow from within him." By this he
meant the Spirit, whom those who believed in him
were later to receive. Up to that time the Spirit had not
been given, since Jesus had not yet been glorified.'

We have a prophecy and a promise that has the
power to create a real hunger and thirst deep within.
Belief then, in Jesus and His word releases the baptism
of the Holy Spirit.

The scriptures give three cautions:

Do not resist the Holy Spirit

Acts 7:51. The first martyr of the faith, Stephen,
says, "You stiff-necked people, with uncircumcised
hearts and ears! You are just like your fathers: You
always resist the Holy Spirit!"

Clearly it was common for the religious people to
resist the truth and it was almost always for the sake of

control. We must not fall into the same trap.

Do not put out the Spirit's Fire

1 Thessalonians 5:12-22. 'Now we ask you, brothers, to respect those who work hard among you, who are over you in the Lord and who admonish you. Hold them in the highest regard in love because of their work. Live in peace with each other. And we urge you, brothers, warn those who are idle, encourage the timid, help the weak, be patient with everyone. Make sure that nobody pays back wrong for wrong, but always try to be kind to each other and to everyone else.

Be joyful always; pray continually; give thanks in all circumstances, for this is God's will for you in Christ Jesus.

Do not put out the Spirit's fire; do not treat prophecies with contempt. Test everything. Hold on to the good. Avoid every kind of evil.

May God himself, the God of peace, sanctify you through and through. May your whole spirit, soul and body be kept blameless at the coming of our Lord Jesus Christ. The one who calls you is faithful and he will do it.

Brothers, pray for us. Greet all the brothers with a holy kiss. I charge you before the Lord to have this letter read to all the brothers.'

I urge you to study this passage with care. It looks as though some of the leaders and older members were not too keen on some gifts the Holy Spirit brings, (prophecy), whilst some of the younger ones were keen on other gifts. Paul calls for respect and asks that the fire of the Spirit should not be put out!

Oh that this teaching was heeded. Do you recognise your own church fellowships here? I recognise almost every church I have ministered in. Take time to learn the lessons of this passage.

Do not grieve the Holy Spirit

Ephesians 4:25-5:21. 'Therefore each of you must put off falsehood and speak truthfully to his neighbour, for we are all members of one body. In your anger do not sin. Do not let the sun go down while you are still angry, and do not give the devil a foothold. He who has been stealing must steal no longer, but must work, doing something useful with his own hands that he may have something to share with those in need.

Do not let any unwholesome talk come out of your mouths, but only what is helpful for building others up according to their needs, that it may benefit those who listen. And do not grieve the Holy Spirit of God, with whom you were sealed for the day of redemption. Get rid of all bitterness, rage and anger, brawling and slander, along with every form of malice. Be kind and compassionate to one another, forgiving each other, just as in Christ God forgave you. Be imitators of God, therefore, as dearly loved children and live a life of love, just as Christ loved us and gave himself up for us as a fragrant offering and sacrifice to God.

But among you there must not be even a hint of sexual immorality, or of any kind of impurity, or of greed, because these are improper for God's holy people. Nor should there be obscenity, foolish talk or coarse joking, which are out of place, but rather thanksgiving. For of this you can be sure: No immoral, impure or greedy person - such a man is an idolater - has any inheritance in the kingdom of Christ and of God. Let no one deceive you with empty words, for because of such things God's wrath comes on those who are disobedient. Therefore do not be partners with them. For you were once darkness, but now you are light in the Lord. Live as children of light (for the fruit of the light consists in all goodness, righteousness and truth) and find out what pleases the Lord. Have nothing to do with the fruitless deeds of darkness, but rather expose them. For it is shameful even to mention what the disobedient do in secret. But everything exposed by the light becomes visible, for it is light that makes everything visible. This is why it is said:

'Wake up, O sleeper,

rise from the dead,

and Christ will shine on you.'

Be very careful, then, how you live - not as unwise but as wise, making the most of every opportunity, because the days are evil. Therefore do not be foolish, but understand what the Lord's will is. Do not get drunk on wine, which leads to debauchery. Instead, be filled with the Spirit. Speak to one another with psalms, hymns and spiritual songs. Sing and make music in your heart to the Lord, always giving thanks to God the Father for everything, in the name of our Lord Jesus Christ.'

If I were to be given £1 for every teaching I have heard about the definition of the word 'Grieve' I would be a wealthy man. All we need to know about grieving the Holy Spirit is to be found in these verses. It is about wrong relationships one with another and the antidotes for it.

This is a quote from David Pytches in his booklet, 'Be filled with the Spirit':

'In the history of the church, almost every spiritual renewal has been preceded by Christians sorting out their relationships with each other: forgiving and asking for forgiveness, turning away from all known sin and seeking to walk in love.'

What an opportunity is ours right now.

3: Hindrances of which we should be aware

Here is a list of ten, in no particular order, (I would invite you to think of others):

Fear

Someone has counted how many times the words 'Fear not' appear in the Bible. It is 366. One for everyday of the year including Leap Year! The words often precede God about to do something good and something new in someone's life!

When I first began to systematically teach about the Holy Spirit people queued up with their lists of fears. Fears about how God might change them, fears about how God would embarrass them, fears about how they might be affected, fears for life changes, fears about friends, even fears about fears. Oh, how the devil loved it, oh how he encouraged it, oh how he delighted in it, oh how he stirred up fear through the church. Do you trust fear or trust God? Have you any reason to believe that God will in anyway hurt you?

Unbelief

John 12:29. 'Then a voice came from heaven, "I have glorified it, and will glorify it again." The crowd that was there and heard it said it had thundered; others said an angel had spoken to him.'

There are always those who will believe it thundered rather than an angel spoke. "Who do you think you are, trying to teach me this?" has also been a response. The gospel, in all its fullness is a new concept, good news, a new belief, today just as it was to Athens and Rome when the Spirit bearers returned home from their epic journey to celebrate the Jewish Festival of Pentecost in Jerusalem. We know thousands believed but we are not told how many thousands did not. When confronted with unbelief we do not stop preaching and teaching, indeed we are spurred on to more.

Unconfessed sin

The Spirit of God is the HOLY Spirit so He is unable to fill the unclean vessel. That is not to say He will not use what is unclean. Indeed He is sovereign. The Bible is full of instances where this occurs. If you think of how God uses you, would you say you are 100% clean on a 24/7 basis? I think not and it is certainly not so in my own case.

However, when we are seeking the in-filling of the Holy Spirit, which we find ourselves doing on a regular basis once baptised in the Spirit, we take time to confess. This is because there is no way that we can clean ourselves. The only way to deal with the 'dirt' in our lives is to confess it, which is naming it to God. Then repent of it, which is turn away from it. Then ask God to reveal what we have overlooked or are not aware of. I well remember doing this when I got really serious about being baptised in the Holy Spirit. Thinking I was through with my confession and repentance I asked God if He had anything to show me. Literally, for the next hour and more (I could not accurately tell) he told me what was sin to Him in my life that went unrecognized by me that He wanted changed. In between bouts of tears and repentance it seemed the whole of my life came under His gaze and my surrender. We are here talking about serious business with the Almighty!

Confusion

Acts 19:1-7. 'While Apollos was at Corinth, Paul took the road through the interior and arrived at Ephesus. There he found some disciples and asked them, "Did you receive the Holy Spirit when you believed?"

They answered, "No, we have not even heard that there is a Holy Spirit."

So Paul asked, "Then what baptism did you receive?"

"John's baptism," they replied.

Paul said, "John's baptism was a baptism of repentance. He told the people to believe in the one coming after him, that is, in Jesus." On hearing this, they were baptised into the name of the Lord Jesus. When Paul placed his hands on them, the Holy Spirit came on them, and they spoke in tongues and prophesied. There were about twelve men in all.'

Notice that this passage of scripture tells us that right from the beginning there was confusion. We cannot contain God in a box. We cannot prescribe His ways. They are past our understanding.

There was and always will be confusion because we are learning of the ways of the Almighty which are far above ours. However, we are exposed to situations that dramatically increase the potential for confusion. The gospel was brought to us by those whose understanding of the ways of, and the working of, the Holy Spirit were flawed. Flawed foundations make for a weak edifice always in danger of collapsing. It is to be seen all around us. Even more so in these days when preachers are going from nation to nation offering a gospel and a gifting of the Holy Spirit which is so often linked to something else. Join our stream; accept our doctrine; learn our prosperity; come and be counted with us and so help to improve our international statistics! Confusion is everywhere and we are often seen as part of it.

As to handling this confusion there seems only one way. It simply has to be a reliance on scripture with understanding guided by the Holy Spirit. If it is not in the Bible avoid it. Where there are those who confuse you with scripture, the need for discernment is vital. There is nothing more successful for the enemy than to sow confusion and it is easy to see how successful he has been.

Complacency

Many of today's Churches and Christians are quite satisfied with where they are. They see no reason to seek to go further with God. They are content and comfortable with things as they are. Where this pertains in a fellowship there is very little that can be done. Without hunger and thirst for God and the knowledge that there is always more, little can ever be achieved. This is of course a denial of the Gospel and the call of Christ to go into all the world. We are called to be fellow workers, not fellow spectators; we are called to participate, not to abstain; we are called to be on the move, not to be stationary. To follow is to be on the move and it is certain that Christ is always on the move. He always wants to move us on from where we are. He is forever calling us forward and onward and wants to facilitate all by the Holy Spirit. Christ is not content to leave us where we are. Why should we be content to stay where we are?

Poor levels of personal commitment

I once heard David Watson, a leader of the renewal ministry in the UK until his untimely death, give a vivid illustration of what commitment is all about. He held a book in his hand and then placed a glove over the wrist of the hand holding the book. He then spoke to the glove telling it to pick up the book. Of course, nothing happened. He then spoke to the glove a second time and said, "Watch me." He picked up the book with his other hand and said this was the way it is done. He had now told the glove what to do and shown the book what to do but still nothing had happened. Does that sound like something God has done? He's told us what to do in his word, shown us what to do in Jesus, but what happens? Nothing! By the Ascension nothing had happened, but then Pentecost changed all that. Once David Watson put his hand in the glove it was empowered to do what is was designed for. It now had the power to 'do'. It picked up the book, no trouble. As the hand fills the glove so the Holy Spirit fills our lives. Now we are free to do what is asked of us, what we are commanded and what the Spirit inspires.

Poor levels of commitment are found when we do not fill the glove with our hand. Not wanting the Spirit is to remain powerless and of little practical value.

Jealousy

Jealousy has the power to paralyze. When we are jealous of what others can do or others can be we become unable to respond as we should. We distance ourselves and find ourselves paralyzed and impotent. We say it is alright for them. If that happens between people it certainly happens between churches. It is destructive, divisive and demeaning.

We have a saying, "The grass is greener on the other side of the fence." It can be like that between churches where the other ministers always seem to work harder and where the Holy Spirit always seems more active. Instead of learning from them, our jealousy makes us critical and we end up being paralyzed and impotent. In reality the grass is greener where it is watered by the Holy Spirit.

Lack of right teaching

The antidote for wrong teaching is not to stop teaching altogether, but rather to put right teaching in place. Let me tell you what I mean. For years many denominations have believed that the Pentecostal teaching about speaking in tongues was wrong. As a result all teaching about tongues was stopped, whereas a better way would have been to provide the churches with right teaching about speaking in tongues! So many churches today suffer from wrong teaching, even from the scriptures. This inevitably leads to all kinds of confusion and wrong attitudes and behaviours. Often what is taught is a denominational 'line' or 'truth' rather than the scripture itself. That can take you down many confusing paths. Let the Bible speak its truth for itself and see what kind of church you have.

Self-centeredness

People, like churches, can become too interested in themselves. That is a very dangerous place to stand. You can come to think of yourself as more important than anyone else and likewise your church more important or significant than any other. What is it that the Bible says?

Romans 12:3. 'For by the grace given me I say to every one of you: Do not think of yourself more highly than you ought, but rather think of yourself with sober judgment, in accordance with the measure of faith God has given you.'

Ephesian 4:29. 'Do not let any unwholesome talk come out of your mouths, but only what is helpful for building others up according to their needs, that it may benefit those who listen. And do not grieve the Holy Spirit of God, with whom you were sealed for the day of redemption. Get rid of all bitterness, rage and anger, brawling and slander, along with every form of malice. Be kind and compassionate to one another, forgiving each other, just as in Christ God forgave you.'

Can you imagine belonging to a church where these truths are taught and these kind of lives lived? What an opportunity for the Holy Spirit!

Ignorance

Have you noticed that it is often the most ignorant

who speak most frequently and often the loudest?

1 Corinthians 12:1-3. 'Now about spiritual gifts, brothers, I do not want you to be ignorant. You know that when you were pagans, somehow or other you were influenced and led astray to mute idols. Therefore I tell you that no one who is speaking by the Spirit of God says, "Jesus be cursed," and no one can say, "Jesus is Lord," except by the Holy Spirit.'

We are not talking about ignorance of subjects taught at school, we are taking about the ignorance of God's word. One of the things that happens when you begin to follow Jesus with an enthusiasm that you have never done before, is that you get an insatiable appetite for God's truth found in his word. You do all you can to get a Bible and when you get one, you do not put it somewhere for people to admire the fact that you have a Bible. You begin to wear it out by reading and studying it.

All these are hindrances to the Holy Spirit being able to make headway in the believer and church. Now it is time for you to try and move ahead some more.

So are you ready to be baptised in the Holy Spirit?

Acts 19:4-6. 'Paul said, "John's baptism was a baptism of repentance. He told the people to believe in the one coming after him, that is, in Jesus." On hearing this, they were baptised into the name of the Lord Jesus. When Paul placed his hands on them, the Holy Spirit came on them, and they spoke in tongues and prophesied. There were about twelve men in all.'

Some suggest that only the apostles laid hands on people but today's experience shows that the Lord responds when others do the same.

He was a Catholic Priest. He had come forward in response to an invitation to receive the Holy Spirit baptism. I happened to be the nearest to him and asked him what he was seeking. "To be filled with the Holy Spirit and to speak in tongues." he responded. So I asked him to stretch out his hands as if to receive a gift and then asked Jesus to baptise him in the Holy Spirit. I laid hands on him as another ministry team member lightly touched his hands. Nothing seemed to happen and so we waited and prayed in tongues. A few moments passed and all that could be heard were the many prayers of the ministry teams as they moved among those seeking a powerful touch from the Spirit. Then suddenly, to our surprise, he began to sing in a beautiful tenor voice, only it was not English, it was in a different tongue! Later we learned that he had longed to be a professional singer but had become a priest. We knew he had been baptised in the Holy Spirit and had sung in the Spirit and so did he.

Often people speak in tongues when they are baptised in the Holy Spirit but it is not always the case. When I was baptised in the Holy Spirit I was alone in my room, on my knees, crying out to God to forgive all my sin and fill me with His Spirit. I knew he had when I spoke in tongues as I had no idea what I was praying. Clearly God did.

Jesus Baptises us with the Holy Spirit when we repent, believe, confess, ask, cry out, hold out our hands, stand, sit, lie down, pray, remain silent, have hands laid on or whatever else shows the condition of our heart that we are serious in our desire, seeking not for ourselves but to be His alone.

At Villa Oulongwe, just over the border from

Malawi in Mozambique, when we invited the Holy Spirit to come on about 20 people, one man spoke in tongues. It was perfect English. An Acts 2 tongue, when we heard him speaking in our own language praising God. He could only speak Chichewa and Portuguese according to his wife and Pastor!

I was with a small group of young pastors who were really seeking God for more of Himself for their Ministry. We stood around and laid hands on each other and the Holy Spirit came among us. Some were filled for the first time others were refilled, but all knew they had been touched by the Holy Spirit. Some fell to the floor, some spoke in tongues, some cried, but all were anointed that morning.

The truth is that Jesus baptises us in the Holy Spirit wherever and whenever he wants to and on an extremely frequent basis. Without his continuous infilling we are restricted to our human gifting and how we happen to feel at any given time.

So let me remind you of what is important if you are seriously going to ask Jesus to keep filling you with the Holy Spirit.

Be sure you are hungry and thirsty for more of God. John 7:37-39. 'On the last and greatest day of the Feast, Jesus stood and said in a loud voice, "If anyone is thirsty, let him come to me and drink. Whoever believes in me, as the Scripture has said, streams of living water will flow from within him." By this he meant the Spirit, whom those who believed in him were later to receive. Up to that time the Spirit had not been given, since Jesus had not yet been glorified.'

Confess and repent of sins known and unknown. Acts 2:38-39. 'Peter replied, "Repent and be baptised, every one of you, in the name of Jesus Christ for the forgiveness of your sins. And you will receive the gift of the Holy Spirit. The promise is for you and your children and for all who are far off - for all whom the Lord our God will call."'

Ask Jesus to baptise and fill you with the Holy Spirit. Wait quietly for Him to visit whether you are alone, in a group, or in the congregation.

4: The gifts of the Holy Spirit

Paul, in his letters to the churches tries to help them understand that water baptism and Spirit baptism are not ends in themselves. They are purpose driven events in the believer's life to equip them for the task of ushering in the kingdom.

Two consequences flow from being baptised in the Holy Spirit and regularly being filled with the Holy Spirit:

- The believer receives gifts

- The believer's life produces certain fruit

There is a formative and foundational scripture that needs to be understood before we launch into a teaching about the gifts:

1 Corinthians 12:1-7. 'Now about spiritual gifts, brothers, I do not want you to be ignorant. You know that when you were pagans, somehow or other you were influenced and led astray to mute idols. Therefore I tell you that no one who is speaking by the Spirit of God says, "Jesus be cursed," and no one can say, "Jesus is Lord," except by the Holy Spirit.

There are different kinds of gifts, but the same Spirit. There are different kinds of service, but the same Lord. There are different kinds of working, but the same God works all of them in all men.

Now to each one the manifestation of the Spirit is

given for the common good.'

When Paul says he does not want the believers to be ignorant about Spiritual Gifts he is saying that it is important and crucial that they are well informed concerning them. That is what this Handbook is all about. He refers to idols that could not speak. Now they know a living Saviour who constantly speaks, which means he can be listened to. Confessing 'Jesus is Lord', as all do at believer's baptism, means the Saviour, through the Spirit, has spoken into our lives, we have heard and responded and are able to make such a confession. In other words Paul is saying you have already heard and responded to the Holy Spirit, but there is more, much more.

He then goes to pains to point out that it doesn't matter which gift or how many gifts you experience, they all come from the one, same Holy Spirit. Again he had a reason for saying this. He did not want any division among believers because of this. More will be said later about this for Paul gives a whole teaching on it. (1 Corinthians 13).

What Paul then says, which is of such tremendous importance, is that every believer has access to all gifts. Let me put it this way. If you are a builder you will have certain tools, if you are a carpenter you will have a different set of tools and if you are a farmer yet another set of tools. As a believer you have a set of tools and it comprises the different gifts of the Spirit to enable you in different situations. The builder, carpenter and farmer will select the right tool needed to complete the particular task that confronts him. So it is with the believer, from among the various gifts he looks for the one most useful for dealing with the issue before him. You do not use all the tools at the same time if you are a builder, carpenter or farmer, neither do you use all the gifts all the time as a believer. You use the right tool for the right job. Sometimes however you will need to use several different gifts to get a job done, just as you would if a builder, carpenter or farmer. We are now going to explore what is in the believer's tool kit!

The following is a list of scriptures that tell us about gifts. We shall explore each in turn.

1 Corinthians 12:8-10. 'To one there is given through the Spirit the message of wisdom, to another the message of knowledge by means of the same Spirit, to another faith by the same Spirit, to another gifts of healing by that one Spirit, to another miraculous powers, to another prophecy, to another distinguishing between spirits, to another speaking in different kinds of tongues, and to still another the interpretation of tongues.'

1 Corinthians 12:28-30. 'And in the church God has appointed first of all apostles, second prophets, third teachers, then workers of miracles, also those having gifts of healing, those able to help others, those with gifts of administration, and those speaking in different kinds of tongues. Are all apostles? Are all prophets? Are all teachers? Do all work miracles? Do all have gifts of healing? Do all speak in tongues? Do all interpret? But eagerly desire the greater gifts.'

Romans 12:3-8. 'For by the grace given me I say to

every one of you: Do not think of yourself more highly than you ought, but rather think of yourself with sober judgment, in accordance with the measure of faith God has given you. Just as each of us has one body with many members, and these members do not all have the same function, so in Christ we who are many form one body, and each member belongs to all the others. We have different gifts, according to the grace given us. If a man's gift is prophesying, let him use it in proportion to his faith. If it is serving, let him serve; if it is teaching, let him teach; if it is encouraging, let him encourage; if it is contributing to the needs of others, let him give generously; if it is leadership, let him govern diligently; if it is showing mercy, let him do it cheerfully.'

Ephesians 4:7-14. 'But to each one of us grace has been given as Christ apportioned it. This is why it says: "When he ascended on high, he led captives in his train and gave gifts to men." (What does 'he ascended' mean except that he also descended to the lower, earthly regions? He who descended is the very one who ascended higher than all the heavens, in order to fill the whole universe). It was he who gave some to be apostles, some to be prophets, some to be evangelists, and some to be pastors and teachers, to prepare God's people for works of service, so that the body of Christ may be built up until we all reach unity in the faith and in the knowledge of the Son of God and become mature, attaining to the whole measure of the fullness of Christ.

Then we will no longer be infants, tossed back and forth by the waves, and blown here and there by every wind of teaching and by the cunning and craftiness of men in their deceitful scheming. Instead, speaking the truth in love, we will in all things grow up into him who is the Head, that is, Christ. From him the whole body, joined and held together by every supporting ligament, grows and builds itself up in love, as each part does its work.'

1 Corinthians 7:7. 'But each man has his own gift from God; one has this gift, another has that.'

1 Peter 4:9-11. 'Offer hospitality to one another without grumbling. Each one should use whatever gift he has received to serve others, faithfully administering God's grace in its various forms. If anyone speaks, he should do it as one speaking the very words of God. If anyone serves, he should do it with the strength God provides, so that in all things God may be praised through Jesus Christ. To him be the glory and the power forever and ever. Amen.'

It is these scriptures that give us the foundation for our teaching about the gifts believers filled with the Holy Spirit can experience. These we shall now explore.

1 Corinthians 12:7 is a key verse when considering the gifts. It says, 'Now to each one the manifestation of the Spirit is given for the common good.' He is making it clear that all the gifts are given for the 'common good'. This means the good of the whole church, all believers. They are not prizes awarded for some kind of meritorious service, rather they are, tools to get a job done. As we have said often gifts are used in combinations or groupings. It's good to be alert for that.

In Greek the gifts are called 'phanerosis' i.e. manifestations of the Spirit. Here is one way of grouping them:

Gifts of Revelation
Word of Wisdom
Word of Knowledge

Gifts of Power
Gifts of Faith
Gifts of Healings
Working of Miracles

Gifts of Communication
Gift of Prophecy
Discerning of Spirits
Speaking in Tongues
Interpretation of Tongues.

5: Gifts of revelation

Word of wisdom

This is a gift of supernatural wisdom given in and for a specific situation. It will be seen to be quite extraordinary and beyond our natural limitations.

It is given for a specific purpose.
It is God's perspective on the situation.
It can unlock a situation and open up a way ahead.

An Old Testament example: **1 Kings 3:16–28**. 'Solomon, the prostitutes and the baby.'

'Now two prostitutes came to the king and stood before him. One of them said, "My lord, this woman and I live in the same house. I had a baby while she was there with me. The third day after my child was born, this woman also had a baby. We were alone; there was no one in the house but the two of us.

"During the night this woman's son died because she lay on him. So she got up in the middle of the night and took my son from my side while I your servant was asleep. She put him by her breast and put her dead son by my breast. The next morning, I got up to nurse my son - and he was dead! But when I looked at him closely in the morning light, I saw that it wasn't the son I had borne." The other woman said, "No! The living one is my son; the dead one is yours." But the first one insisted, "No! The dead one is yours; the living one is mine." And so they argued before the king.

The king said, "This one says, my son is alive and your son is dead, while that one says, no! Your son is dead and mine is alive." Then the king said, "Bring me a sword." So they brought a sword for the king. He then gave an order: "Cut the living child in two and give half to one and half to the other." The woman whose son was alive was filled with compassion for her son and said to the king, "Please, my lord, give her the living baby! Don't kill him!" But the other said, "Neither I nor you shall have him. Cut him in two!" Then the king gave his ruling: "Give the living baby to the first woman. Do not kill him; she is his mother." When all Israel heard the verdict the king had given, they held the king in awe, because they saw that he had wisdom from God to administer justice.'

Think how this meets these three criteria.

It is given for a specific purpose.
It is God's perspective on the situation.
It can unlock a situation and open up a way ahead.

A New Testament example: **Matthew 21:23–27**. 'From whom is John's baptism?'

'Jesus entered the temple courts, and, while he was teaching, the chief priests and the elders of the people came to him. "By what authority are you doing these things?" they asked. "And who gave you this authority?"

Jesus replied, "I will also ask you one question. If you answer me, I will tell you by what authority I am doing these things. John's baptism - where did it come from? Was it from heaven, or from men?"

They discussed it among themselves and said, "If we say, 'From heaven,' he will ask, 'Then why didn't you believe him?' But if we say, 'From men' – we are afraid of the people, for they all hold that John was a prophet."

So they answered Jesus, "We don't know."

Then he said, "Neither will I tell you by what authority I am doing these things.'"

Think how this meets the three criteria:

It is given for a specific purpose.
It is God's perspective on the situation.
It can unlock a situation and open up a way ahead.

Another New Testament example: **Matthew 22:15 – 22**. 'Caesar's inscription on the coin.'

'Then the Pharisees went out and laid plans to trap him in his words. They sent their disciples to him along with the Herodians. "Teacher," they said, "we know you are a man of integrity and that you teach the way of God in accordance with the truth. You aren't swayed by men, because you pay no attention to who they are. Tell us then, what is your opinion? Is it right to pay taxes to Caesar or not?"

But Jesus, knowing their evil intent, said, "You hypocrites, why are you trying to trap me? Show me the coin used for paying the tax." They brought him a denarius, and he asked them, "Whose portrait is this? And whose inscription?"

"Caesar's," they replied. Then he said to them,

"Give to Caesar what is Caesar's, and to God what is God's." When they heard this, they were amazed. So they left him and went away.'

Another; **Mark 2:27-28.** 'The Sabbath.'

'Then he said to them, "The Sabbath was made for man, not man for the Sabbath. So the Son of Man is Lord even of the Sabbath."'

Think how these meet the three Criteria:

It is given for a specific purpose.
It is God's perspective on the situation.
It can unlock a situation and open up a way ahead.

Here are some contemporary examples:

In our congregation a pastor asked me for prayer for his son who had lost his way and was into drugs. I asked the Lord how I should pray. I sensed the Holy Spirit say to ask that someone would be sent across the young man's path and would challenge him. We prayed that prayer and the pastor said he would go on praying the prayer. Twelve months later the pastor returned to our congregation and found me. He told me that another young man had crossed his son's path and had so challenged him that now his son was drug free and back with the Lord.

In Mzuzu, Malawi, a lady had walked five kilometers to attend our meetings because she heard we prayed for the sick. She arrived after the meetings were over and we were going back to Lilongwe the next day. I suggested that the people there could pray as effectively as any of the team and that they should do so. However, they insisted that I go with three others from the team. We entered the home and there she was, sitting in a chair. As I looked at her the Spirit said to me do not touch her, just watch. I sensed the Lord was going to do something. I told the team to watch. As we did so we saw her stomach convulse and she seemed very uncomfortable. This lasted about five minutes. I asked her to lay her hand on her stomach and we each in turn touched her hand as it lay on her stomach. It seemed to be vibrating. In a few more minutes she declared that God had healed her sick stomach. She had suffered for five years with terrible pains. Four years later I was told the story of how she was still testifying to God's healing that night and preaching Jesus in the open air to all who cared to listen. Over time she had won hundreds for the kingdom!

Think how these meet the three Criteria:

It is given for a specific purpose
It is God's perspective on the situation
It can unlock a situation and open up a way ahead

Word of knowledge

This is supernatural revelation of FACT about a person or situation about which you had no knowledge in your natural mind. It is often only a fragment of knowledge that God wants you to know to enable you to minister in a given situation more effectively. It may have to do with the past, present, or the future and is used to build up, edify, encourage, disclose, bless, expose, reveal, and release.

2 Kings 6:9–12. 'A warning of an enemy's plans for destruction.'

'The man of God sent word to the king of Israel: "Beware of passing that place, because the Arameans are going down there." So the king of Israel checked on the place indicated by the man of God. Time and again Elisha warned the king, so that he was on his guard in such places. This enraged the king of Aram. He summoned his officers and demanded of them, "Will you not tell me which of us is on the side of the king of Israel?"
"None of us, my lord the king," said one of his officers, "but Elisha, the prophet who is in Israel, tells the king of Israel the very words you speak in your bedroom."'

Think how this meets the criteria:

Build up
Edify
Encourage
Disclose
Bless
Expose
Reveal
Release

Acts 16:9. 'An indication of a man's need.'

'During the night Paul had a vision of a man of

Macedonia standing and begging him, "Come over to Macedonia and help us.'"

Think how this meets the criteria:

Build up
Edify
Encourage
Disclose
Bless
Expose
Reveal
Release

Acts 10:17–23. 'A revelation of a visitor coming who had not yet arrived.'

'While Peter was wondering about the meaning of the vision, the men sent by Cornelius found out where Simon's house was and stopped at the gate. They called out, asking if Simon who was known as Peter was staying there. While Peter was still thinking about the vision, the Spirit said to him, "Simon, three men are looking for you. So get up and go downstairs. Do not hesitate to go with them, for I have sent them." Peter went down and said to the men, "I'm the one you're looking for. Why have you come?" The men replied, "We have come from Cornelius the centurion. He is a righteous and God-fearing man, who is respected by all the Jewish people. A holy angel told him to have you come to his house so that he could hear what you have to say." Then Peter invited the men into the house to be his guests.'

Think how this meets the criteria:

Build up
Edify
Encourage
Disclose
Bless
Expose
Reveal
Release

A word of knowledge can be any of the following: a revelation of what God is doing; a detail about a person, to release them from suffering; or instruction on how to pray for the sick.

Now for some contemporary examples:

I sensed the Lord speaking to me and saying, "Tell the lady in the blue dress I want to minister to her." I spoke this to the congregation as it was dispersing. Remember we said that often words of knowledge come only as fragments. One of the stewards came hurrying up to me and said a lady in a blue dress was waiting to see me. When we met I told her I thought God wanted to minister to her in some way. Through her tears she said that she had just walked out on her husband, turned into the church, didn't know where she was going but never wanted to see her husband again. The Lord touched her heart and she went home to her husband. In time they were reconciled, joined the church and now live together happily in their retirement.

I recall the first time I asked the Lord for a word of

knowledge. This is what my spirit seemed to hear God say, "I will give you a word of knowledge but it will be for my glory and not your ego!" It was sometime before I asked again.

Often the word of knowledge is not a 'word' so much as a pain and you know it does not belong to you. You ask if anyone owns such a pain and if they do often the Lord will touch them and heal them.

Every time I went near a certain lady in a meeting tears would well up in my eyes. After it happened two or three times I realised the Lord wanted to say something to me about her so I asked her. Her reply was a shock to me. She told me she had been diagnosed at the hospital with a rampant cancer and had only a few weeks to live. She was only twenty years old. The Lord did not say He wanted to heal her but we helped her to make a peaceful death because he wanted her to be healed in heaven.

Think how these examples match what we said at the beginning:

Build up
Edify
Encourage
Disclose
Bless
Expose
Reveal
Release

Now share examples you have experienced and see how they relate to what you are being taught.

6: Gifts of power

Gifts of Faith

There are four kinds of faith mentioned in the New Testament. You need to know what they are and use them appropriately.

Faith that is a CREED: This relates to the beliefs we hold.

Ephesians 4.13. '....Until we all reach unity in the faith and in the knowledge of the Son of God and become mature, attaining to the whole measure of the fullness of Christ.'

Jude 1:3. 'Dear friends, although I was very eager to write to you about the salvation we share, I felt I had to write and urge you to contend for the faith that was once for all entrusted to the saints.'

An example of this faith is; "I believe in One God, Father, Son and Holy Spirit."

Faith that is the basic TRUST we have in God: This is Saving Faith.

John 3:16. 'For God so loved the world that he gave his one and only Son, that whoever believes in him shall not perish but have eternal life.'

It is a fact that we believe to be true.

Faith that is a FRUIT of the Spirit: This cultivates loyalty in the life of a believer.

Galatians 5:22. 'But the fruit of the Spirit is love, joy, peace, patience, kindness, goodness, faithfulness, gentleness and self-control.' (More of this below).

It is the quality of a believer being steadfast.

Faith that is a GIFT of the Spirit: This is a mountain-moving surge of faith that gives incredible confidence to speak and often brings things into being.

Matthew 17:20. 'I tell you the truth, if you have faith as small as a mustard seed, you can say to this mountain, "Move from here to there" and it will move. Nothing will be impossible for you.'

Matthew 21:21. 'I tell you the truth, if you have faith and do not doubt, not only can you do what was done to the fig tree, but also you can say to this mountain, "Go, throw yourself into the sea," and it will be done.'

1 Corinthians 13.2. 'If I have the gift of prophecy and can fathom all mysteries and all knowledge, and if I have a faith that can move mountains, but have not love, I am nothing.'

We are talking about faith that is a gift of the Spirit. It is often a direct supernatural blessing that brings fulfilment to human words that carry God's promises.

Genesis 27:28. 'May God give you of heaven's dew and of earth's richness - an abundance of grain and new wine.' This is Isaac blessing his son Jacob. Look at Hebrews 11:1-2. 'Now faith is being sure of what we hope for and certain of what we do not see. This is what the ancients were commended for.'

Hebrews 11:3-20. 'By faith we understand that the universe was formed at God's command, so that what is seen was not made out of what was visible. By faith Abel offered God a better sacrifice than Cain did. By faith he was commended as a righteous man, when God spoke well of his offerings. And by faith he still speaks, even though he is dead.

By faith Enoch was taken from this life, so that he did not experience death; he could not be found, because God had taken him away. For before he was taken, he was commended as one who pleased God. And without faith it is impossible to please God, because anyone who comes to him must believe that he exists and that he rewards those who earnestly seek him.

By faith Noah, when warned about things not yet seen, in holy fear built an ark to save his family. By his faith he condemned the world and became heir of the righteousness that comes by faith.

By faith Abraham, when called to go to a place he would later receive as his inheritance, obeyed and went, even though he did not know where he was going. By faith he made his home in the promised land like a stranger in a foreign country; he lived in tents, as did Isaac and Jacob, who were heirs with him of the same promise. For he was looking forward to the city with foundations, whose architect and builder is God.

By faith Abraham, even though he was past age - and Sarah herself was barren - was enabled to become a father because he considered him faithful who had made the promise. And so from this one man, and he as good as dead, came descendants as numerous as the stars in the sky and as countless as the sand on the seashore.

All these people were still living by faith when they died. They did not receive the things promised; they only saw them and welcomed them from a distance. And they admitted that they were aliens and strangers on earth. People who say such things show that they are looking for a country of their own. If they had been thinking of the country they had left, they would have had opportunity to return. Instead, they were longing for a better country - a heavenly one. Therefore God is not ashamed to be called their God, for He has prepared a city for them.

By faith Abraham, when God tested him, offered Isaac as a sacrifice. He who had received the promises was about to sacrifice his one and only son, even though God had said to him, "It is through Isaac that your offspring will be reckoned." Abraham reasoned that God could raise the dead, and figuratively speaking, he did receive Isaac back from death.

By faith Isaac blessed Jacob and Esau in regard to their future.'

The gift of Faith can be seen in so many of the events of the Old Testament, in Daniel's trials, Elijah's adventures, Elisha's exploits, Jesus' ministry, Paul's service and so on.

Hebrews 11:6. 'And without faith it is impossible

to please God, because anyone who comes to him must believe that he exists and that he rewards those who earnestly seek him.'

All Spirit filled believers find the truth of this very quickly.

Now for some contemporary examples:

As a church we believed God had promised us some dilapidated buildings to turn into a centre to care for women suffering abuse or domestic violence and to care for families under stress. To do this would cost three quarters of a million British pounds sterling. I was afraid. Then God gave me a gift of faith to give to the church. He showed me the end of a rainbow, which is so unusual that we had to stop the car and make sure our eyes were not deceiving us. Then in my spirit, God said, "Tell my people what I have promised, that will I do." Come Sunday I told the assembled congregation and we rejoiced. In three years everything was paid for, completed and working!

The wife of a leader from a church in Mozambique was barren and the families wanted her to seek the potions of the witch doctor. One of our team received the gift of faith and declared that by the same time next year she would have a child. When we visited the following year she brought a beautiful baby girl to see us. Since then the family has grown and she now has four children!

Consider how these examples relate to the 'surge' of faith that we spoke of and provide your own examples.

Gifts of healings

These gifts give us access to the divine healing so often encountered in the New Testament. They are a fundamental sign of the in-breaking of the kingdom that Jesus came to inaugurate; the will done in heaven touching earth, as we so often pray when we say the Lord's Prayer.

This healing is straight from the heart of God and is available because of what Christ did on the cross.

Isaiah 53:4-6. 'Surely he took up our infirmities and carried our sorrows, yet we considered him stricken by God, smitten by him, and afflicted. But he was pierced for our transgressions, he was crushed for our iniquities; the punishment that brought us peace was upon him, and by his wounds we are healed.'

Matt 8:16–17. 'When evening came, many who were demon-possessed were brought to him, and he drove out the spirits with a word and healed all the sick. This was to fulfil what was spoken through the prophet Isaiah:

"He took up our infirmities and carried our diseases."'

1 Peter 2:24. 'He himself bore our sins in his body on the tree, so that we might die to sins and live for righteousness; by his wounds you have been healed.'

The gifts of healings seem often to work in conjunction with the whole range of other gifts.

A critical verse for healing is **John 5:19.** 'The son can do nothing by himself: He can only do what he sees the Father doing.'

If the sense of the presence of the Lord is very apparent then there is always a potential for healing to take place. Sometimes it just happens, as the Lord is present in worship. Sometimes a single person is used, at other times almost everyone is involved one way or another. Sometimes people stand in a line seeking healing at other times healing takes place where people are. Sometimes it is quick, but it is always a process.

Therefore there is no special way to pray or declare a healing, no special place, and no special person.

It is just a sovereign God who delights to set his children free. The really fun thing is He gives us all a chance to play. (Another quote from the late John Wimber.)

Biblical healings abound and instead of giving many quotes open your Bible at any one of the gospels and beginning with the first chapter see how long it takes you to find a healing.

Now for some contemporary examples of healing:

Mrs Smith (that is not her real name) had suffered with back pain for many years. Often it was so bad she would have to leave her work at the hospital and return home. We were attending a healing service. Those who felt they needed prayer were invited to stand in the aisles. Those next to them were invited to lay hands where people declared pain. I asked Mrs Smith where her pain was and she said in her upper backbone, so I laid one hand there. Suddenly her backbone began to vibrate so much that my hand was vibrating as well. I was so amazed that I called people to come and touch my hand to experience what the Lord was doing. She has never had the pain again.

God loves to visit his people when they praise and

worship Him. Psalm 22:3 'Yet you are enthroned as the Holy One; you are the praise of Israel', is often translated as, 'Yet you are holy, enthroned on the praises of Israel.' Worship is God's appointed way for divine meeting!

Before the time for worship the leader said that when we had finished he would ask for testimonies from the congregation asking how God had been encountered and he particularly encouraged us to be open to healing. The time came and testimonies were asked for. The first to his feet, with an unsteady walk, was an elderly man. "How have you been healed?' he was asked. This was his reply: "When I came into this building tonight I could only see out of my left eye. Now I can see out of my right eye just as clearly!"

She had just come back from the funeral of her uncle, about 5 kilometers away from her home village. Her husband had asked her to return the next day, but she stayed on a week.

Her husband brought her to a small meeting we were holding in a school hall where a church was being planted in a remote district in Malawi. He asked us to pray for her because she had returned from her uncle's funeral as a 'different woman' - and he thought the uncle's spirit had possessed her. She looked very sad and unhappy. We asked if we could pray for her and she said it would be fine. As we approached her she stood up and ran away at a furious pace. We thought we would never see her again. However her husband and friends found her whilst we were having lunch and encouraged her to return to allow us to pray. This time she did not run away. We invited the Holy

Spirit to descend and overwhelm her. (Doing this will often provoke any other spirit present to manifest). She leapt from the chair, threw herself on the floor and began to roll around in circles, so much so that at first we had to jump over her! Commanding the spirit to leave in the name of Jesus, after a few minutes we helped her back to her chair. She was healed and her husband received his wife as one restored from the dead. We then prayed for her and asked the Lord to come and completely fill her body and every part of her life with His compassionate love. (This is often a good way to conclude any sort of deliverance).

We had crowded meetings for three days and we were soon to return to Lilongwe. We asked the assembled host to do one final thing. We asked them to stand together and cry out to God for whatever healing they or their friends were in need. Cry out they did and nearly thirty minutes passed before we could interact with them again. Those who had been touched by God were asked to raise their hands. A whole sea of hands were raised, more raised than not. We left that village believing that God had touched and healed many.

Notice that Paul talks both of 'gifts', plural and 'healings', plural. This suggests that there are hosts of gifts and hosts of healings and every Spirit filled believer can pray for the sick though none of us can heal anyone. If there is any healing, it is all of God. He is the only one who can heal, as he is the one who made us. We ask Him to do the healing. This takes us straight into the territory of the enemy and one of his weapons is fear. He hates us to believe God can heal. He hates us to ask God to heal and he will do anything to undermine our faith. He will tell us we fail and he is right because, I say again, only God can heal. He will tell us we have not been healed and he will instruct his legion of demons to mess us about as much as possible. Demons flee at the name of Jesus. YOU have the authority to speak the name of Jesus. Tell satan and his demons that a place has been prepared for them and to leave the scene where you are praying.

This is sometimes called spiritual warfare and that is what it is.

Working of miracles

This is the rule of God in heaven breaking in and touching the earth. **Matthew 6:10**. 'Your kingdom come, your will be done on earth as it is in heaven.'

Where heaven touches earth, there the perfect will of God is done, so miracles are inevitable!

Miracles often happen in the context of the COMPASSION and MERCY of Jesus, for example, take the greatest miracle of all, the resurrection of Jesus. Heaven collides with earth. That is right out of the Father's heart demonstrating his compassion for our fallen condition. The ministry of the Holy Spirit is to make this real to us here and now.

Yet who can say how or when? If God calls upon you to command a miracle then without hesitation give the glory to Him and command it.

I had listened to a lecture on spiritual gifts. It had come to an end with a ministry time and this was now over. From behind me a lady came, entering the room in a wheel chair. She made her way through the crowd around the speaker. She had missed the session but wanted to ask a question of the speaker.

He did no more than look at her and say to her, "Stand up". To the amazement of those nearby she stood up and from that day has never used the wheel chair again, over twelve years ago and counting!

My son's father-in-law used a wheel chair for many years and whilst in it he planted three churches. Countless people said they had a word for him that God would heal him. Countless people told him to stand up. He was never healed and died in his chair. He was just over forty years of age.

What did I learn from this? Be ready, in season and out, and never, never say what you would like to happen, command it in the name of Jesus, and believe!

The Bible is full of illustrations. Here I list a few for you to read.

John 2:1-11. (Jesus changes water into wine).

'On the third day a wedding took place at Cana in Galilee. Jesus' mother was there, and Jesus and his disciples had also been invited to the wedding. When the wine was gone, Jesus' mother said to him, "They have no more wine."

"Dear woman, why do you involve me?" Jesus replied, "My time has not yet come."

His mother said to the servants, "Do whatever he tells you."

Nearby stood six stone water jars, the kind used by the Jews for ceremonial washing, each holding from twenty to thirty gallons.

Jesus said to the servants, "Fill the jars with water"; so they filled them to the brim.

Then he told them, "Now draw some out and take it

to the master of the banquet."

They did so, and the master of the banquet tasted the water that had been turned into wine. He did not realise where it had come from, though the servants who had drawn the water knew. Then he called the bridegroom aside and said, "Everyone brings out the choice wine first and then the cheaper wine after the guests have had too much to drink; but you have saved the best till now."

This, the first of his miraculous signs, Jesus performed in Cana of Galilee. He thus revealed his glory, and his disciples put their faith in him.'

John 11:38-44. (Jesus raises the dead).

'Jesus, once more deeply moved, came to the tomb. It was a cave with a stone laid across the entrance.

"Take away the stone," he said.

"But, Lord," said Martha, the sister of the dead man, "by this time there is a bad odour, for he has been there four days."

Then Jesus said, "Did I not tell you that if you believed, you would see the glory of God?"

So they took away the stone. Then Jesus looked up and said, "Father, I thank you that you have heard me. I knew that you always hear me, but I said this for the benefit of the people standing here, that they may believe that you sent me."

When he had said this, Jesus called in a loud voice, "Lazarus, come out!" The dead man came out, his hands and feet wrapped with strips of linen, and a cloth around his face.

Jesus said to them, "Take off the grave clothes and let him go."'

Mark 1:32-34. (Many healed and demons dealt with).

'That evening after sunset the people brought to Jesus all the sick and demon-possessed. The whole town gathered at the door, and Jesus healed many who had various diseases. He also drove out many demons, but he would not let the demons speak because they knew who he was.'

Have I ever performed a miracle? That is the wrong question. Has God ever produced a miracle through me? Yes, many times over. For the greatest miracle of all is when a person passes from darkness to light, is born again, becomes a believer, and becomes the place where the Holy Spirit dwells.

7: Gifts of communication

Prophecy

This is a special ability, which God gives to any or all the members of the Body of Christ to receive and communicate an immediate message from his heart to his gathered people or to any individual wherever you meet them.

It is not fortune telling neither is it telling the future. Sometimes though it can do both. It is always telling forth the heart of God as the Holy Spirit equips you.

It has little or nothing to do with Old Testament prophecy. Remember in those days the Holy Spirit was only available to the very few whom God chose and anointed. The Joel Prophecy fulfilled at Pentecost changed all that.

The New Testament makes it clear that the purpose of prophecy is threefold. **1 Corinthians 14:3**. 'But everyone who prophesies speaks to men for their strengthening, encouragement and comfort.'

It is to strengthen
It is to encourage
It is to comfort

This gift is to be eagerly desired. **1 Corinthians 14:1**: 'Follow the way of love and eagerly desire spiritual gifts, especially the gift of prophecy. Therefore, my brothers, be eager to prophesy.'

The secret of prophecy is hearing the voice of God. God is never silent. (Even in the seeming silence He is speaking.) He is trying to attract our attention all of the time. If He cannot do it one way He will do it another. How many are the ways you use to attract someone's attention? God uses many, many more. So wake up, watch out, look and listen.

Expect Him to speak to you in every situation.

Be careful! You don't have to tell it all and you need the gift of wisdom to know what and how to share.

Infrequently this is a message from God that contains information which will give people a choice. Agabus is an example:

Acts 11:28. 'One of them, named Agabus, stood up and through the Spirit predicted that a severe famine would spread over the entire Roman world. (This happened during the reign of Claudius).'

Acts 21:10-14. 'After we had been there a number of days, a prophet named Agabus came down from Judea. Coming over to us, he took Paul's belt, tied his own hands and feet with it and said, "The Holy Spirit says, in this way the Jews of Jerusalem will bind the owner of this belt and will hand him over to the Gentiles."

When we heard this, we and the people there pleaded with Paul not to go up to Jerusalem. Then Paul answered, "Why are you weeping and breaking my heart? I am ready not only to be bound, but also to

die in Jerusalem for the name of the Lord Jesus."
When he would not be dissuaded, we gave up and
said, "The Lord's will be done.""

Paul is made aware of what is going to happen and
chooses to embrace it and not avoid it as he was
advised.

Now for some contemporary examples:

A meeting had been arranged where two of us
would be teaching about the Holy Spirit. Earlier in the
day I saw a young man holding a bunch of keys in his
hands hurrying around. The Holy Spirit enabled me to
remember him, so in the meeting I asked the Lord, (in
my spirit) did it have any significance? I asked the
young man to stand (which was a real act of faith) and
there was a gasp from the congregation. It turned out
to be the pastor's son. I felt God had a word for him.
In the moment I had no idea what it was but I began to
speak and God gave the word. The keys represented a
means of unlocking people's lives with the truth of the
gospel and he would most likely train for the ministry.
Four years later I was at another meeting when a
young man I didn't know came up to me and told me
he was training for the ministry. He told me that I had
prophesied that over him. I had forgotten him, he had
not forgotten me. God had got him!

It was the first Sunday of the year and I wanted to
hear something special from the Lord for the people.
In the communion service I started to see different
colours resting on people. I knew a little about colours
and their meaning but I have learned a lot more since.

The colours enabled me to encourage them for the coming year.

I wrote the following to help someone who wanted to know more about colour in scripture:

Symbolic Colours

Gold/Amber
The glory of God, heaven. (Ezekiel 1:4. 8:2. Revelation 21:18).

Black
Death, famine, divine judgment. (Lamentations 4:8. Revelation 6:5. Deuteronomy 4:11. Zechariah 6:2. Revelation 6:12).

Blue
Heaven, heavenly, revelation, obedience; water baptism, Holy Spirit. (Exodus 26:36. Numbers 4:11. Numbers 15:38, 40. Revelation 9:17).

Crimson
Blood atonement, sacrifice. (Leviticus 14:52. Joshua 2:18, 21. Isaiah 1:18).

Purple
Kingship, royalty, highest status. (John 19:2. Judges 8:26).

Red
War, bloodshed, wisdom, anointing, power. (Revelation 6:4. 12: 3. 2 Kings 3:22).

Scarlet

Sin, blood atonement, sacrifice. (Isaiah 1:18. Leviticus 14:52).

White

Purity, light, righteousness. (Isaiah 1:18. Revelation 6:2. 7:9. 19:8).

Green

Peace, pasture, rest, growth and prosperity. (Psalm 23).

Rainbow

Promises that are being kept. (Genesis 9:16).

Often colours come in combinations and sometime they are woven together. See Exodus 26:1.

Also remember the maxim that the things of the Spirit invariably begin in the natural. Sometimes a close awareness of the colours of God's creation can pay dividends. It is always wise to make sure that your interpretation is consistent with scripture. If it cannot be found in scripture, handle with great care.

Sometimes the Holy Spirit will make us aware of colours attendant upon a person or persons. I well remember a New Year day when He invited me to call out about a dozen people, each of whom, for me, had a colour around them. It turned out that the colour was God's way of getting my attention and there was a word of prophecy about the coming year for each of them all related to the colour.

A final example before you begin to think of your own experiences in this area:

In one of the village meetings the Lord drew my

attention to a lady sitting a few rows from the front. The Lord got my attention through her headdress which was a type I had not seen before. The Lord gave me no clue to what he wanted to say until I asked the lady to stand. Then the Lord started to tell me about an increase in her responsibilities in the church she attended that was coming her way. (After giving a word to someone I always pray for them straight away). I then moved on to another man sitting almost at the back. Again I asked him to stand. There was a gasp and laughter! Asking why this was so, I found that it was the husband of the lady I had just prophesied over and he had just become a pastor of a fresh church. The Lord had several words of encouragement for him.

All prophecy must be carefully weighed. **1 Corinthians 14:31-32**. 'For you can all prophesy in turn so that everyone may be instructed and encouraged. The spirits of prophets are subject to the control of prophets.' What this implies is the words of the prophet are subject to him and should be able to stand the scrutiny of others.

The basic rules are simple. Does what is said in any way contradict scripture? If it does it is false. Does it condemn? If it does it is false. Does it strengthen, encourage, or comfort? If it does the chances are it might be from God.

Here is a way that I have used to teach people to prophesy.

I gather people sitting in a circle so that everyone has someone sitting to their left and right. One person starts by asking the next their name. Round you go until everyone knows the name of the person on their right and left. The second move is to take it in turns to say something affirming about the person, but the sentence must begin with the words, GOD says (name) you are.... for example, loved. So each speaks a known truth from God into the next person's life. The third move is similar, but must begin with (name) God wants you to know.... for example, how much He cares for you. Round the circle you go each saying something different to the next person. Now you invite the Holy Spirit to give you a word for your neighbour. After a short pause to listen to the Spirit the fourth move begins, (name) I think the Lord is saying to you....

It is amazing how this can unlock Gods words to us and I have seen some prophecies shared by folk who would never have dreamed they could prophesy.

Why not try this in a group?

Discerning of spirits

This is the spiritual gift that enables you to discern the motivating spirit behind words, deeds, actions and situations.

This is the gift where you carefully weigh all that is said and done. It is one of the most needed gifts for every believer, but at the same time it is one of the most ignored.

There are only three sources behind any word or deed.

The Divine option: God is setting it all up and

working everything together.

The demonic option: Satan is setting it all up and manipulating everything.

The human option: You are doing it. It is out of your flesh.

Of course there is a fourth option and that is where there is a combination of two or more of the above options.

1 Corinthians 2:4-5. 'My message and my preaching were not with wise and persuasive words, but with a demonstration of the Spirit's power, so that your faith might not rest on men's wisdom, but on God's power.' Paul is saying we all have the ability to evaluate what is being said.

Discernment is the weighing of what is said.

I have always found that it is wise to ask the Holy Spirit with what you are dealing.
Here are two examples, one from my early days of ministry and one from my last visit to Malawi.

It was eleven o'clock in the evening when the phone rang. It was a call from a nurse who attended the church. She was attending a Bible study group in a friend's house with other nurses. About nine in all. "Can you come now?" was her urgent plea. Asking what the problem was things soon became clear. Apparently a young man was manifesting a demon, behaving like a dog, and frightening the whole group.

Needless to say I went, knocked on the door and was taken into the hall. Before entering the room I was trying to think what I might do. My experience of casting out demons was somewhat limited. The door of the room was opened for me. As I entered this young man behaving like a dog, jumped at me using his hands as paws and knocked me against the wall! That was the moment I came to my senses and said, under my breath, 'What am I dealing with here Lord?' To which the answer came straight back into my mind, 'You are not dealing with demons!' The gift of discernment had come to my rescue and there would be no dramatic deliverances that night. Aware that there were a number of very impressionable youngsters there, I looked at the guy who had jumped at me and in a loud voice, (I am not sure why) I said, 'Shut up, sit down and stop playing the fool'. He moved quickly to sit down and looked somewhat taken aback.

To cut a long story short, this was not the first time he had behaved this way. In this, and in other groups, it seemed as though he was trying to frighten or impress nurses. I told him the Spirit had revealed to me that he had never been inhabited by a demon; that the reason he behaved like this was to draw attention to himself; though many had tried to cast his demon out all failed because there was not one there. I took him back to his flat, prayed that Jesus would come and bring peace, that the Holy Spirit would enable him to sleep and that the Father would heal him of the need to behave in this way.

He slept like a baby, started to follow Jesus in a more appropriate way and never played with the demonic all the years I continued to know him.

This taught me a big lesson about discernment. He had been to two professionals whom I greatly respected but who had been helpless to do anything for him.

So now my number one rule is seek discernment in everything. Ask the Holy Spirit what you are dealing with.

The meeting had ended and we were making our way to the vehicle when we were called back. A mother had brought her child and asked if we would cast out the demon which was making her behave badly, including telling people in the village when the witches were coming!

There were crowds of people around. The first thing we did was to find a quiet place away from everyone where we could do what needed to be done in private and maintain the young girl's dignity and self esteem. There were five in our team plus two local pastors and the overseer.

Quietly I spoke to this group and said ask the Holy Spirit to tell you if there are any demons here. I gave them a few moments to pray silently and then asked them, one by one, has the Holy Spirit said anything about demons to you? Use the gift of discernment. All said they had heard nothing about demons. Next we asked the Holy Spirit to come on the girl and in a few moments began to ask questions. Once more to cut the long story short we uncovered the fact that she had been sent to live with her grandmother in another village to help get water and food when she needed it. Her grandmother was visited by two women, one the little girl liked, because she was kind and another that she hated and of whom she was afraid. This one turned out to be a witch who was trying to train the little girl

78

to be an apprentice witch! We prayed for her, gave her mother some instructions, advised her pastor what to do and left.

The Spirit of discernment had been present through the Holy Spirit and had come to our rescue.

Now is the time to talk with others about some of your experiences and see what you are beginning to learn about discernment.

Speaking in tongues

Baptism in the Holy Spirit can be, and often is, accompanied by many different experiences. One of these is a spontaneous bubbling up and release of some sounds that defy our rational understanding. A kind of language we don't always understand. It is something that every believer can anticipate, and in which every believer can participate, but not all do. It is a gift available for all and not for the select few. However, it has often been taught out of us like other gospel truths because satan makes them so divisive.

Here we are talking about inspired, spontaneous utterance generated by the Holy Spirit in a language, spoken or sung, that is entirely unlearned by the speaker.

What follows is very important to grasp. There are three distinct manifestations of this gift, each clearly revealed in the New Testament.

Firstly, an utterance which is not understood by the speaker, but is overheard by the public and without interpretation is discovered to be someone's native language. Acts 2:4-8 'All of them were filled with the Holy Spirit and began to speak in other tongues as the Spirit enabled them. Now there were staying in Jerusalem God-fearing Jews from every nation under heaven. When they heard this sound, a crowd came together in bewilderment, because each one heard them speaking in his own language. Utterly amazed, they asked: "Are not all these men who are speaking Galileans? Then how is it that each of us hears them in his own native language? Parthians, Medes and Elamites; residents of Mesopotamia, Judea and Cappadocia, Pontus and Asia, Phrygia and Pamphylia, Egypt and the parts of Libya near Cyrene; visitors from Rome (both Jews and converts to Judaism); Cretans and Arabs - we hear them declaring the wonders of God in our own tongues!" Amazed and perplexed, they asked one another, "What does this mean?"'

We have heard Chichewa speaking people declaring the praises of God in perfect English but they had no idea what they were saying!

Secondly, a public utterance in worship that is not understood as a known language and must be followed by an interpretation given by the Holy Spirit to someone else, or less often to the speaker themselves. 1 Corinthians 14:27-28. 'If anyone speaks in a tongue, two or at the most three should speak, one at a time, and someone must interpret. If there is no interpreter, the speaker should keep quiet in the church and speak to himself and God.'

This message usually is some kind of praise song to Jesus that glorifies God. It is not an admonition to the congregation. (See what we said about prophecy).

Thirdly, the use of tongues in private worship which needs no interpretation. 1 Corinthians 14:4. 'He who speaks in a tongue edifies himself.' Though according to 1 Corinthians 14:13 it is quite alright to ask for an interpretation. 'For this reason anyone who speaks in a tongue should pray that he may interpret what he says.' Paul said he prayed in tongues more than anyone. 'I thank God that I speak in tongues more than all of you.' 1 Corinthians 14:18. He also talked about singing in the Spirit. 1 Corinthians 14:15. 'I will pray with my spirit, but I will also pray with my mind; I will sing with my spirit, but I will also sing with my mind.'

Use this gift in worship, public or private, as well as very frequently through the day. It is edifying, encouraging and often enlightening to your own soul.

These are the three most important manifestations of this gift whose purpose is to edify. Jude 1:20-21: 'But you, dear friends, build yourselves up in your most holy faith and pray in the Holy Spirit.' 1 Corinthians 14:4: 'He who speaks in a tongue edifies himself.' 1 Corinthians 14:5: 'I would like every one of you to speak in tongues.'

This gift also enables the church to function as a body when used in public. Different members speak different messages and other members receive interpretations. Many get to participate.

It is another clear sign of the presence of the kingdom of God in the midst. 1 Corinthians 14:22. 'Tongues, then, are a sign, not for believers but for unbelievers': By this we understand unbelievers will be made aware of the presence of God. Acts 2:12. 'Since you are eager to have spiritual gifts, try to excel in gifts that build up the church.'

Interpretation of tongues

This is a supernatural revelation through the Holy Spirit that enables a believer to communicate in the language of the listeners the essence of what has been said in a tongue, when the church has come together. Why not ask, when you come together, if anyone senses God is giving them a tongue?

Interpretation is not translation. It is just as much a supernatural gift as the tongue itself.

Receiving this gift is apparent when you hear the tongue being spoken and the very sense of what is being said is there in your mind.

If prophecy is a message from God to his people then most often a tongue is that which is offered to God from the heart of his people and the interpretation will reflect this. However, there are exceptions and sometimes the tongue is a prayer and/or a prophecy but this is more the exception rather than the rule. This is because when the Holy Spirit is dispersing gifts among God's people some get one, some get another and some get several. We don't have to be able to accurately describe or define every gift. From time to time they will merge, they will overwhelm us and our human understanding will be found wanting. But, as Paul says, 'The stranger in the midst will know that God is there.'

All these gifts are from the Father's treasure store and must be handled in a way that honours Him and gives Him all the glory.

It is part of the leader's responsibility to pastor these gifts with love and encouragement.

It is the duty of every believer to allow this process and to grow into maturity in the gifts of the Spirit.

8: Learning to minister in the gifts of the Holy Spirit

Whatever God does the enemy (satan) will attempt to copy and he is able.

Avoid giving people good advice; there are other times and places for that. If you sense God is saying something then say, "I think God maybe saying…"

We come now to look at **1 Corinthians 12:28-30**. 'And in the church God has appointed first of all apostles, second prophets, third teachers, then workers of miracles, also those having gifts of healing, those able to help others, those with gifts of administration, and those speaking in different kinds of tongues. Are all apostles? Are all prophets? Are all teachers? Do all work miracles? Do all have gifts of healing? Do all speak in tongues? Do all interpret? But eagerly desire the greater gifts.'

Already we have explored some of the gifts mentioned here, so now we shall look at what is new to us. We come to the provision God makes for His Church.

These verses introduce us to the fact that God gives certain 'offices' as gifts to help enable His church to function. Named here are 'apostles', 'prophets' and 'teachers'. There is also mentioned Gifts of 'administration'. These gifts help the church function smoothly and wise leaders are always on the look out for people with such gifts.

But let us look a little more closely at the offices mentioned. Notice the scripture does not say that each church or for that matter any church should appoint apostles, prophets and teachers. What the church looks for are people whose Christian lives show that they have such gifts. You are an apostle, prophet, or teacher because you show signs of doing the job, not because people in the church think you might be good at it. God gives the gifts, it is your job to look for them, recognise them and give them their rightful place within the congregation. It has nothing to do with appointing but everything to do with agreeing with God and that is done through recognition.

Romans 12:3-8. 'For by the grace given me I say to every one of you: Do not think of yourself more highly than you ought, but rather think of yourself with sober judgment, in accordance with the measure of faith God has given you. Just as each of us has one body with many members, and these members do not all have the same function, so in Christ we who are many form one body, and each member belongs to all the others. We have different gifts, according to the grace given us. If a man's gift is prophesying, let him use it in proportion to his faith. If it is serving, let him serve; if it is teaching, let him teach; if it is encouraging, let him encourage; if it is contributing to the needs of others, let him give generously; if it is leadership, let him govern diligently; if it is showing mercy, let him do it cheerfully.'

This passage will pay great dividends if studied carefully for it says so much about how the gifts should be used in the church. But, our focus is the gifts and here we find yet more new ones mentioned.

The gift of serving

There is no doubt that everyone in a congregation has the ability to serve. But those who are gifted by the Holy Spirit to serve stand out for all to see. The congregation blesses them. I know a congregation where they wanted to recognise deacons. They looked around the congregation to find those already doing the job displaying gifts in serving. They found six and the following Sunday they had a recognition time in the service for them, where they brought them to the front and blessed them as gifts from God to the congregation.

The gift of encouraging

Acts 4:36. 'Joseph, a Levite from Cyprus, whom the apostles called Barnabas (which means Son of Encouragement)'.

Here is the perfect example of what we are talking about. A man named Joseph exhibits the gift of 'encouragement' so the apostles actually change his name to 'encourager'. That's how this thing works. You don't appoint an encourager. You look to see who is doing it and then give him/her the recognition.

The gift of giving

Again, when the church comes together everyone brings some sort of gift. All give but there are those who exhibit the gift of generosity, and they give over and above what everyone else does or could do. So, you do not 'appoint' the generous person in the church. You are glad to recognise and bless the one gifted with generosity. Note, it is not always the one who gives the most who is the most generous. (You might wish to look up Mark 12:41-44, which describes the extravagant generosity of a poor widow).

The gift of leadership

Congregations are often appointing leaders instead of recognizing them. Here again the truth is the same. We look to see whom the Lord is gifting with leadership. We do not pick the loudest voice; the most important in the community; the one who pushes themselves forward; we look to see whom God is anointing. Sometimes they do not last long. (Look at the story of Stephen).

The gift of showing mercy

She, I say she, because it is often women who are able to receive this gift in a way that the men do not seem so able, will rarely be found alone. She will always seem to have a group of others with her and they want to be near so that some of her mercy will rub off on them.

Ephesians 4:7-14. 'But to each one of us grace has been given as Christ apportioned it. This is why it says:

'When he ascended on high, he led captives in his train and gave gifts to men.' (What does 'he ascended' mean except that he also descended to the lower, earthly regions? He who descended is the very one who ascended higher than all the heavens, in order to fill the whole universe.) It was he who gave some to be apostles, some to be prophets, some to be evangelists, and some to be pastors and teachers, to prepare God's people for works of service, so that the body of Christ may be built up until we all reach unity in the faith and in the knowledge of the Son of God and become mature, attaining to the whole measure of the fullness of Christ.

Then we will no longer be infants, tossed back and forth by the waves, and blown here and there by every wind of teaching and by the cunning and craftiness of men in their deceitful scheming. Instead, speaking the truth in love, we will in all things grow up into him who is the Head, that is, Christ. From him the whole body, joined and held together by every supporting ligament, grows and builds itself up in love, as each part does its work.'

This passage adds two more 'offices' that the Lord gives to the church to enable it to function as he would have it. It brings the total to five and so you may have heard folk talk about the Five Fold Ministry. The two additions here are 'evangelists' and 'pastors', which go to complete the list. Should every congregation look to have these five Holy Spirit offices among them? No, but they should be looking regularly to see who the Holy Spirit is gifting in their midst and remember the key is so often the people who are doing the job. Often pastors are seen as having one or more congregations to look after. Apostles, prophets, teachers and evangelists more often seem to work with multiple congregations but remember they are all rooted in a congregation. This cannot be given too much emphasis as the world wide church today seems to suffer from self appointed folk claiming the 'offices' to themselves, and they are sometimes cut off from local congregations. Did you know that before Jimmy Carter became President of the USA, he would do his utmost to be in church on Sunday to teach his Sunday School Class? When he became President he made a promise which he kept, that no one staying in the White House over night would leave without hearing the Gospel, and that included every world leader who stayed with him. National, maybe; international, sometimes; local, always. That is how God plans His church.

1 Corinthians 7:7. 'But each man has his own gift from God; one has this gift, another has that.'

This verse underlines for us, 'everyone gets to play' as John Wimber was so fond of saying.

1 Peter 4:9-11. 'Offer hospitality to one another without grumbling. Each one should use whatever gift he has received to serve others, faithfully administering God's grace in its various forms. If anyone speaks, he should do it as one speaking the very words of God. If anyone serves, he should do it with the strength God provides, so that in all things God may be praised through Jesus Christ. To him be the glory and the power forever and ever. Amen.'

This is a great conclusion to our excursion through the gifts and once more I commend it as a passage to be explored together in a group. It describes the character the Holy Spirit is trying continuously to work into us.

1 Corinthians 12, which talks about the gifts of the spirit, and 1 Corinthians 14, which puts the gifts in the

context of the body at worship, have between them 1 Corinthians 13.

This is a chapter that has often been torn out of its context and used for the marriage ceremony. Paul is not talking about a wedding. He is talking about the context for the right use of the gifts the Holy Spirit distributes just as the Father wills.

This chapter defines 'the way of love.' If Paul found he needed to define it in his day when teaching about the gifts of the Spirit, how much more do we need to heed what is being said here today?

Here we are helped to understand how we need to behave as we use the gifts. The gifts are given to build up the Body. Satan, well aware of the power of the gifts, has devised a brilliant strategy to cripple their use in the church and thereby stunt its growth. He makes sure that they are high-jacked to fringe and cult groups. So successful has he been that the mainstream denominational churches have said this is much too controversial an area for us to become involved. They say we will ignore 1 Corinthians 12 and 1 Corinthians 14, but 1 Corinthians 13 is lovely! We will keep this for something special like when couples get married. Crafty satan!

However, Paul says: 'And now I will show you the most excellent way…' (1 Corinthians 12:31); and this is about using the spiritual gifts the Father gives His children.

Paul also says; 'Now you are the body of Christ and each one of you is a part of it,' (1 Corinthians 12:27), and he continues; 'But eagerly desire the greater gifts.' (1 Corinthians 12:31).

The church in Corinth was in somewhat of a mess but instead of saying, "I can't teach about the gifts here," Paul said that it was just the place for him to do it. Spiritual gifts are God's way of 'equipping the saints,' which Paul talks about in his letter to the Ephesians.

"I can talk my head off in tongues but if I don't have any love, it's nothing."

"I can have gifts of prophecy, wisdom and knowledge but without love it is nothing."

"I can have the gift of faith and miracles but without love it is all wasted."

"I can give up everything I have and then be martyred and it's all a waste of time and space without LOVE!"

LOVE IS:
    Patient
    Kind
    Does not envy
    Does not boast
    Is not proud
    Is not rude
    Is not self-seeking
    Not easily angered
    Keeps no record of wrongs
    Does not delight in evil
    Rejoices in the truth
    Always protects
    Always trusts

Always hopes
Always perseveres
Never fails

Everything else will fade and fall away. Now we know everything through our fallen human nature that will only be fully redeemed in heaven. Consequently we cannot see at all clearly or hear with accurate precision.

Hang in there! You have Faith, you have Hope, and you have Love. The greatest of these is Love. So let's go for it! Here is how it should be among you!

So it is that Paul continues setting out the context for the use of gifts. They can never be earned. They can never be bought. They are not badges for the best. They are not just for leaders. They are for every believer to help them participate in building up the body of Christ and bringing in the kingdom. That is why the phrase, 'when you come together' is so important. In the midst the Holy Spirit will manifest His presence.

When we come together no one can stand outside the authority of God's anointed leader of His church. For me, when I am in Malawi, or anywhere else for that matter, it is the local pastor. I am in submission to him.

Whatever gifting you may manifest from time to time you are always under the authority of your God appointed leader. You may be more gifted, you may have more wisdom, your gift of prophecy may be greater, and it matters not. Do not step out from under the covering of the leader God has appointed. You are totally exposed and the enemy may attack you. The pastor is there to pastor you whatever the level of your gifting or his. He is going to pastor you no matter how visible you are in the church.

9: Fruits of the Holy Spirit

Baptism in the Holy Spirit is followed by the availability of the Gifts of the Spirit, and now there is a potential for the Fruit of the Spirit to begin to be formed. These have the potential to grow and begin to come to maturity.

Galatians 5:22. 'The fruit of the Spirit is love, joy, peace, kindness, goodness, faithfulness, gentleness, and self-control.'

John 3:3. 'In reply Jesus declared, "I tell you the truth, no one can see the kingdom of God unless he is born again."'

As the Holy Spirit comes to live within the life of a believer certain changes begin to take place. Take that illustration John used to describe coming to faith in Jesus. He said it is like being born again. At the moment of your conception a cell division/ multiplication began to take place and look what happened in the next 9 months. Does something any less miraculous happen when a believer is born again?

2 Corinthians 5:17. 'Therefore, if anyone is in Christ, he is a new creation; the old has gone, the new has come!'

Paul describes the believer as a new creation! Is that not what a babe in Christ is? Now baptised in the Holy Spirit another transformation begins which is followed by another set of consequences.

John 15:1–8. "I am the true vine, and my Father is

the gardener. He cuts off every branch in me that bears no fruit, while every branch that does bear fruit he prunes so that it will be even more fruitful. You are already clean because of the word I have spoken to you. Remain in me, and I will remain in you. No branch can bear fruit by itself; it must remain in the vine. Neither can you bear fruit unless you remain in me. I am the vine; you are the branches. If a man remains in me and I in him, he will bear much fruit; apart from me you can do nothing. If anyone does not remain in me, he is like a branch that is thrown away and withers; such branches are picked up, thrown into the fire and burned. If you remain in me and my words remain in you, ask whatever you wish, and it will be given you. This is to my Father's glory, that you bear much fruit, showing yourselves to be my disciples."

This passage talks about Jesus as the vine and His followers being the branches. Common to both the vine and the branches is the sap that gives the life. I understand the sap to be the Holy Spirit. It is branches that bear fruit as a result of the life pulsing through from the vine. These fruit are grapes. If you visit a vineyard after the flowers are set, listen very carefully for you may hear them groaning and straining to produce grapes. Right or wrong? Wrong! It is a natural process that happens as a result of what a vine is. So is the fruit in the life of the Spirit filled believer. The fruit you see and experience happens because of who you are in Christ. No amount of straining and groaning will produce the fruit in your life.

Love

This is the same unconditional love that Jesus

showed us through laying his life down to save us and is now being exhibited in our lives. It is a process not an immediate accomplishment. It grows and develops, as we become more Christ-like. The final perfection of this fruit will only be apparent in heaven in the very presence of Christ who will change us into His likeness. Is it any wonder people loved to hang out with the followers of Jesus then and now?

Joy

Not the frothy happiness, lightness of spirit, giggly stuff, but rather something so much deeper. It is the joy that enables you still to stand at the very last when everything else has been shaken and fallen away. John 16:20 holds the key: 'Now is your time of grief, but I will see you again and you will rejoice, and no one will take away your joy.' It is that underpinning joy on which the whole of our life as a believer is based. Foundational joy that enables the weak to be strong in the Lord.

Peace

John 14.27. 'Peace I leave with you; my peace I give you. I do not give to you as the world gives. Do not let your hearts be troubled and do not be afraid.' Clearly this is peace that is the possession of Jesus and is the result of the Holy Spirit bearing fruit in His life. This He gives to us and as the Holy Spirit lives within us this peace begins to manifest. The word I like to use to describe this peace is 'stability'. When everything around has come apart and all is chaos the believer bearing this fruit is totally calm. The last days of Jesus illustrate this for us in a very graphic way.

Kindness

Again the life of Jesus exhibits this fruit. His kindness to everyone is so apparent in the lives of all He met. What marks this kindness out as a fruit of the Spirit? Surely it is the fact that, like His love, it is quite unconditional! It is not deserved. It is not earned. It is there to be received. As the Holy Spirit lives out through you watch to see these fruit come to life. You cannot manufacture them. As you grow in the things of the Spirit you watch them mature in your life. Most certainly others do!

Goodness

Moses asked to see God's Glory. **Exodus 33:18 – 19**. 'The Lord said he would cause all His goodness to pass in front of him.... but you cannot see my face ....' The Goodness of the Lord is His self-disclosure through all His visible activity, which is energized by the Holy Spirit. 'And God saw that it was good.' Creation; resurrection; salvation; eternal life; all this activity of God on behalf of His children is His goodness. The goodness, which is the fruit of the Spirit, is all this reflected through our lives into the lives of others. It is not 'being good.' It is becoming Christ-like!

Faithfulness

In our human strength and weakness it is impossible

to be faithful in every respect to God. He is divine and we are human. However, the Holy Spirit works in us and the gift of faithfulness begins to come to life. It is to be received and not earned. It is freely given and not achieved. Revelation 2:10 'Be faithful, even to the point of death, and I will give you the crown of life.' This is received through the Holy Spirit and not achieved through our striving and effort.

Gentleness

To see this fruit beginning to be formed and then ripened in our lives is to discover that we are becoming more like Jesus day by day.

Philippians 2:1–11 is a word picture of our character marked with gentleness. It is a passage to be read but more importantly it is a passage to be lived:

'If you have any encouragement from being united with Christ, if any comfort from his love, if any fellowship with the Spirit, if any tenderness and compassion, then make my joy complete by being like-minded, having the same love, being one in spirit and purpose. Do nothing out of selfish ambition or vain conceit, but in humility consider others better than yourselves. Each of you should look not only to your own interests, but also to the interests of others. Your attitude should be the same as that of Christ Jesus: Who, being in very nature God, did not consider equality with God something to be grasped, but made himself nothing, taking the very nature of a servant, being made in human likeness. And being found in appearance as a man, he humbled himself and became obedient to death - even death on a cross! Therefore God exalted him to the highest place and gave him the name that is above every name, that at the name of Jesus every knee should bow, in heaven and on earth and under the earth, and every tongue confess that Jesus Christ is Lord, to the glory of God the Father.'

Self Control

Having tried it a thousand times I have never once been continuously successful. If you ever have, please let me into the secret. However, what I readily admit to is the fruit of the Holy Spirit found in me from time to time giving me what I would describe as supernatural self-control. It is often the most disarming attitude to find yourself clothed in. I have found myself asking where did that come from? Because it was clear that it had nothing to do with my own resources. In the teaching of Jesus it is hinted at in 'turning the other cheek'. In the life of Jesus its supreme moment is focused in the words, 'Father forgive them they do not know what they are doing.'

Visit and revisit the passages of scripture quoted above. They contain the words of life.

Conclusion

Let us consider the marks of maturity, and try to keep in step with the Holy Spirit.

Galatians 5:25. 'Since we live by the Spirit, let us keep in step with the Spirit.'

First comes our confession of faith in Jesus which is marked by our baptism in water. Second comes our baptism in the Holy Spirit, which is marked by gifts which begin to produce fruit. Third comes our continual filling by the Holy Spirit, which is marked by the beginning of our maturing process. This is simply a basic pattern for everyday life. Let me tell you a story.

When I was 18 years old I was called by the government to report to the barracks to serve king and country. There were forty of us in our intake, young men from all walks of life. In conversation we began to talk together about what we did. However, there was one young man who didn't have to speak a word to tell us what he did. Everyday we saw what he did by what he did. He was a ballet dancer. Everyday he had a dance routine to go through. If he did not, his muscles would seize up, he would quickly be unable to make all of his moves, and that would be the end of his dancing career. His daily dance routine, quite separate from everything else we were called to do, had to be done. So it is for the believer. He has a daily routine that is essential for sustaining and growing his life as a believer. Without its continual practice he soon discovers how unfit and helpless he becomes.

The following, I suggest, is a believer's routine.

Daily Devotion

This is a celebration of all that has been accomplished by Christ, which gives us focus for the day.

Daily Direction

This is an audience with the King that refocuses our life.

Daily Discernment

This is our request to the Holy Spirit for us to walk with Him, and to ask Him to enable us to do everything the Father is asking and disclosing.

So, I end where I began:

The Holy Spirit now is everything to the believer that Jesus was to the disciples then.

Postscript

The Sin against the Holy Spirit

Here are three passages of scripture that cause some Christians a great deal of bother as in some way they think they have committed such a sin and will thereby never find forgiveness:

Matthew 12:31 - 32.

'And so I tell you, every kind of sin and slander can be forgiven, but blasphemy against the Spirit will not be forgiven. Anyone who speaks a word against the Son of Man will be forgiven, but anyone who speaks against the Holy Spirit will not be forgiven, either in this age or in the age to come.'

Mark 3, 28 -29.

'Truly I tell you, people can be forgiven all their sins and every slander they utter, but whoever blasphemes against the Holy Spirit will never be forgiven; they are guilty of an eternal sin.'

Luke12:8-10.

'I tell you, whoever publicly acknowledges me before others, the Son of Man will also acknowledge before the angels of God. But whoever disowns me before others will be disowned before the angels of God. And everyone who speaks a word against the Son of Man will be forgiven, but anyone who blasphemes against the Holy Spirit will not be forgiven.'

My assumption is that these are three accounts of the similar things that Jesus said either only once, or from time to time. It is their interpretation that is of real significance and I can do no better than quote the writing of Louis Berkhof:

'The sin consists in the conscious, malicious and wilful rejection and slander, against evidence and conviction of the testimony of the Holy Spirit respecting the grace of God in Christ, attributing it out of hand and enmity to the Prince of Darkness.... in committing that sin man wilfully, maliciously, and intentionally attributes what is clearly recognized as the work of God to the influence and operation of Satan.' (*Systematic Theology* by Louis Berkhof, the Banner of Truth Trust, 1971; and Berkhof is also quoted in *Systematic Theology* by Wayne Grudem, Inter-Varsity and Zondervan, 1994).

Grudem continues, 'Berkhof explains that the sin itself consists, "Not in doubting the truth, not in a sinful denial of it but in a contradiction of it that goes contrary to the conviction of the mind, to the illumination of the conscience, and even to the verdict of the heart."

The fact that the unpardonable sin involves such extreme hardness of heart and lack of repentance indicates that those who fear they have committed it, yet still have sorrow for sin in their heart and desire to seek after God, certainly do not fall in the category of those who are guilty of it. Berkhof says that, "We may be reasonably sure that those who fear they have committed it and worry about this, and desire the prayers of others for them, have not committed it.'"

Some books that have helped me

'**An Introduction to Pentecostalism**' Global Charismatic Christianity (Introduction to Religion) by Allan Heaton Anderson (Cambridge University Press, 2014)

'**To the Ends of the Earth - Pentecostalism and the Transformation of World Christianity**' (Oxford Studies in World Christianity) by Allan Heaton Anderson (Oxford University Press, 2013)

'**I Believe in the Holy Spirit**' by Michael Green (Hodder and Stoughton, 1975)

'**When Heaven invades Earth**' by Bill Johnson, (Destiny Image Publisher Inc. 2005)

'**Hosting the Presence - Unveiling Heaven's Agenda**' by Bill Johnson (Destiny Image Publisher Inc. 2012), foreword by Heidi Baker

'**Silver to Gold - A journey of Young Revolutionaries**' by Jennifer A. Miskov (Silver to Gold, 2009)

'**Spirit Flood - Rebirth of Spirit Baptism for the 21st Century**' by Jennifer A. Miskov (Silver to Gold, 2010)

'**Life on Wings - The Forgotten Life and Theology**

of Carrie Judd Montgomery' by Jennifer A. Miskov (CPT Press, 2012)

'Come Holy Spirit' by David Pytches (Hodder & Stoughton Religious, 1985)

'Be filled with the Spirit' by David Watson, (A Falcon Booklet, Kingsway Publications, 1982)

'Power Evangelism' by John Wimber and Kevin Springer (Hodder and Stoughton, 2009)

'Power Healing' by John Wimber and Kevin Springer (HarperSanFrancisco, 2009)